IMAGES
of America

HAMMONASSET BEACH STATE PARK

This 1927 view of Hammonasset Beach State Park includes, from left to right, Tom's Creek, Dowd's Point Road (Beach Road) camping, the Grand Pavilion, the Administration Building, the Clam Shed, Short Term Camps above the Clam Shed, and the paid parking area. Meigs Point can be seen at upper right and the Clinton Harbor and Hammonasset River are at top center. (Courtesy of the State of Connecticut Department of Energy and Environmental Protection.)

On the Cover: This 1920s view shows people on the boardwalk and Grand Pavilion enjoying a day at Hammonasset Beach State Park. It was common practice for men to dress in suits, ties, and hats and women in dresses, hats, and coats. (Courtesy of the State of Connecticut Department of Energy and Environmental Protection.)

IMAGES
of America

HAMMONASSET BEACH STATE PARK

Brian Noe and Shelby Docker

ARCADIA
PUBLISHING

ISBN 978-1-4671-2536-9

Published by Arcadia Publishing
Charleston, South Carolina

Printed in the United States of America

Library of Congress Control Number: 2016953985

For all general information, please contact Arcadia Publishing:
Telephone 843-853-2070
Fax 843-853-0044
E-mail sales@arcadiapublishing.com
For customer service and orders:
Toll-Free 1-888-313-2665

Visit us on the Internet at www.arcadiapublishing.com

Dedicated to the commissioners, staff, friends, and volunteers who overcame significant challenges over the past 100-plus years to make over two miles of beautiful coastal Connecticut available to the public to make and share memories for generations to come.

Contents

ACKNOWLEDGMENTS

Our first thanks go to our readers who, by purchasing this book, are contributing to the Friends of Hammonasset, a nonprofit organization that raises funds to directly support Hammonasset Beach State Park.

The authors thank all the individuals and organizations who contributed to this book directly and indirectly, old and new friends, family and strangers, and those who, although no longer here, are able to share their story through photographs, drawings, memorabilia, and writings saved and preserved by family members, historical societies, and archivists.

Special thanks to the people of the State of Connecticut Department of Energy and Environmental Protection (DEEP) past and present who had the vision to record and protect the history of Hammonasset Beach State Park. DEEP greeted us with warmth and cooperation, and without question, made the most significant contribution to this book.

Robert Klee, Commissioner of DEEP
Susan K. Whalen, Deputy Commissioner of DEEP
Alan Levere, Historian of DEEP
Christine Koster, President, Friends of Hammonasset
Don Rankin, Friends of Hammonasset, for his expertise in Native American history and archeology
Charlotte L. Evarts Memorial Archives Inc. of Madison, Connecticut (CLEMA) Board of Directors, Archivist Nancy Bastian
Madison Historical Society (MHS)
Michael Schreiber, Shore Line Trolley Museum in East Haven, Connecticut
Timothy C. Visel, for his research related to Hammonasset Beach State Park
Ralph Lewis, former State Geologist of Connecticut
Gary Nolf, President of the World Atlatl Association
Jeff Barske and family, for Jeff's vintage car expertise and longtime Hammonasset campers
Gail Najarian and family, longtime Hammonasset campers
The editors and publishers at Arcadia for their expertise helping us ensure quality work and the success of this book.

Unless otherwise noted, all images appear courtesy of the State of Connecticut Department of Energy and Environmental Protection.

INTRODUCTION

We grew up and first met at Hammonasset Beach State Park in the summers of the 1960s and 1970s camping with our families, and we still enjoy spending our summers at Hammonasset. Recently we became interested in the history of Hammonasset and were filled with many questions. Who were the visionaries who created the state park system and Hammonasset Beach State Park? When were the pavilions we played on, the nurse's station we ran to after getting stung by jellyfish, and the boardwalks we ran on, biked on (against the rules), and hunted for loose change under built? The economist in me wondered how the park commissioners obtained the resources to expand and keep the park functioning during the Depression. Was Hammonasset really a US Army Air Force base during World War II, as we had heard from some longtime campers?

After researching the topic, we were amazed to discover that there was little in the way of a complete history of Hammonasset. Therefore, we decided to do our best to compile the information we discovered to bring the history of Hammonasset to you.

The stories of the 1920s, 1930s, and 1940s are somewhat lost due to the lack of recorded detail from that era, but please consider the following: While viewing the images presented here, with the captions to understand the story, take a moment to put this book down and imagine the people relaxing and playing on the beach, children crabbing at the creek and riding their bikes, and families enjoying a campfire. Then think back to images and people doing the same since the very first day Hammonasset opened to the public in 1920. Relive the memories of youth, and provide your children the opportunity to make lifelong friends with memories that transcend time. Remember the summer romance and heartbreak, and the freedom to "own the park" in a safe environment surrounded by wonderful people (and the occasional character).

We start with the glaciers that shaped New England and Long Island and the rising seas that filled in what is now Long Island Sound. Ever wonder how the Hammonasset Native Americans lived and survived thousands of years ago?

Let us introduce you to the visionaries who created the state park system and its flagship park, Hammonasset. These men volunteered their time from the 1910s into the 1940s rallying each other against relentless, sometimes hostile, opposition and challenges that most would walk away from. Did you know that one commissioner was able to step up and save Meigs Point from being purchased by private developers?

Try to keep up with the dizzying speed of land acquisition, the determination to complete the purchases, and the moving of cottages in order to complete the park. Discover how the beachfront was developed and why. Find out about the history of the camps and how the commission dealt with inadequate funding in the 1910s and 1920s, only to be pummeled by the Great Depression. And finally, end your tour with the hurricane of 1938, which devastated the park, and the park's quick rebound for the 1939 summer season before becoming a US Army Air Force training base in 1942.

The early decades of Hammonasset Beach reflected the social and economic changes of the time, a theme that continues to this day. Get to know how the visitors and campers lived and enjoyed Hammonasset during this period. Be amazed that the camping community included those with a tent camping next to a luxury trailer, with a mixture of different ethnic groups and immigrants. We were able to confirm folklore, discover new facts, and blow up myths to help you be a Hammonasset expert around the campfire.

We also acknowledge that there are some who know more about the specific history of the park. There are images and stories that we were unable to uncover. We expect to be challenged on some of our facts and stories; this is as it should be. What we share with you is a work in progress with the hope that others complement and supplement this book to provide a more accurate and complete history for all to appreciate. We found that for the answer to some questions and the completion of some stories, we are 10 years too late to unearth history that only those who lived Hammonasset in the early years could tell.

Enjoy these pictures that bring the park to life, and use your imagination to dream about life at Hammonasset in the 1920s, 1930s, and pre–World War II years of the 1940s.

One

The Way Back Machine

There are two compelling questions many have asked about Hammonasset Beach State Park. Why is Meigs Point so rocky when the rest of Hammonasset is so flat and sandy, and who were the Hammonasset Native Americans? Over the past two million years, at least four glaciers have sculpted the bedrock surface of New England and Long Island. This chapter shares how the last two of these glaciations, known as the Illinoian (approximately 190,000 to 130,000 years ago) and Wisconsinan (approximately 85,000 to 11,000 years ago), formed the features of Hammonasset and how Meigs Point's two moraines formed.

Traces of man in the Hammonasset Beach State Park area date back 6,000 to 7,000 years, although it is generally accepted that people lived in the area almost 10,000 years ago. During dredging operations in 1955, Stone Age arrowheads, quartz scrapers, and sharp knives of uniform size and shape were uncovered and deposited on the beach. The Hammonasset and Pilot's Point camps are believed to be the oldest Native American campsites in the area.

When European settlers arrived in the early 1600s, the Hammonasset (meaning "where we dig holes in the ground") Native Americans numbered over 100. They were typical Eastern Woodland farmers subsisting on corn, beans, squash, fish, and game. The Hammonasset tribe lived and farmed in the Hammonassett River area during the summer months, moving to the more densely wooded Durham-Killingworth area for protection in the winter.

Native Americans did not have a written language. European settlers used several Hammonasset spellings, including Athammonassuck and Homonasset, before evolving into Hammonassett. The two-T spelling can be found in some early state park documents and signage. Hammonasset with one T is now universally used as the accepted spelling.

Due to soil that forms slowly, settlement over Native American prime sites, and consistent natural disasters over many centuries, archaeologists are challenged to find Native American artifacts in southern New England. This chapter provides the geology along with actual artifacts and replicas showing how the Hammonasset and neighboring tribes may have lived.

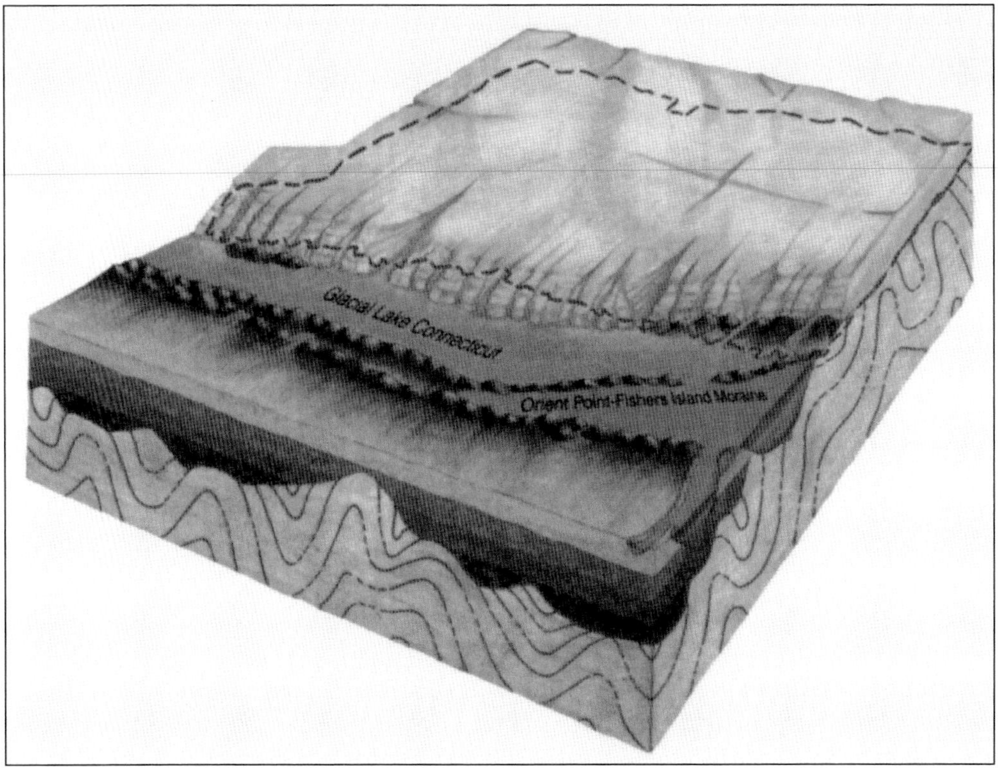

The Wisconsinan glacier was melting back (above Glacial Lake Connecticut) around 21,000 years ago after reaching its terminal point 60 to 70 miles south of today's Long Island. Around this time, the Hammonassett moraines were deposited during pauses in glacial meltback. Glacial Lake Connecticut was dammed in by the Orient Point–Fishers Island moraine. (Courtesy of the Long Island Sound Resource Center and DEEP.)

Faulkner's Island is a drumlin (elongated hill in the shape of an inverted spoon) island composed of glacial till thought to be of the Illinoian glacier age around 140,000 years ago. As the Wisconsinan glacier advanced towards Long Island, it smoothed over this earlier till deposit, creating the drumlin. The flat beach illustrates how wave action has cut into the original hill. (Courtesy of Brian Noe; Keith Hall, pilot.)

This photograph (not at Hammonasset) shows the layers of a typical delta deposit. As the Wisconsinan glaciers receded, meltwater streams flowing across the newly exposed land delivered sediment to Glacial Lake Connecticut. This is how the coastal glacial deltas, like the one at Hammonasset, were built. (Courtesy of Ralph Lewis.)

Unsorted glacial debris (boulders, cobble, and sediment) makes up the moraine at Meigs Point. The fine component of the moraine (sediment) is removed by wave action, forming a cobble/boulder beach, as seen here. These people, like many others, enjoy climbing on the rocks. The second moraine hill near Clinton Harbor is in the background.

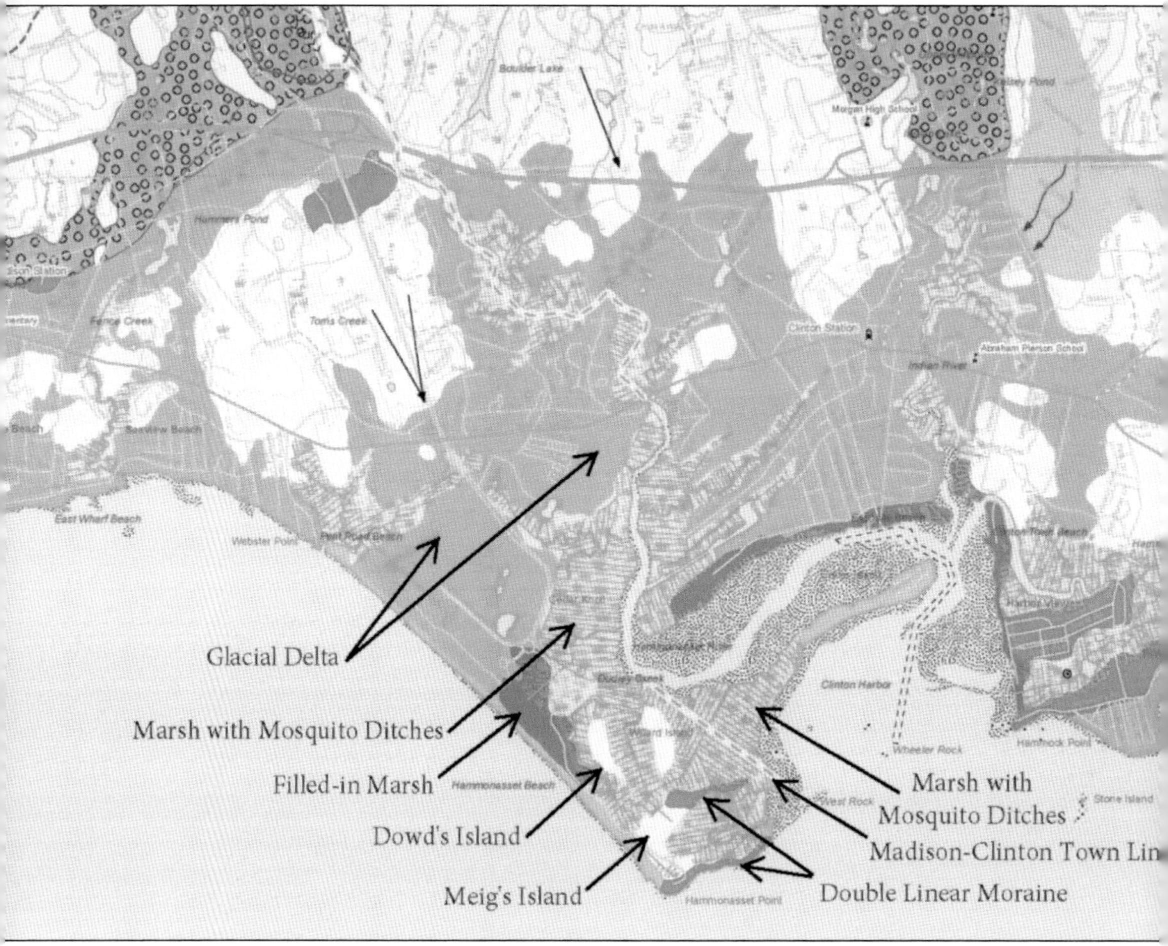

This map, detailing the Quaternary period (glacial and modern geology), shows the extent of the glacial delta, the double linear moraine ridges, and till cropping out at Willard's Island. Dowd's Island is to the left of Willard's; Meigs Island is in between the moraine ridges. As the glacial meltback continued, from about 21,000 to about 19,500 years ago, meltwater streams carried sediment southward to Lake Connecticut. At Hammonasset, the delta that built into the lake was so large that it completely buried the bedrock. As rising Long Island Sound waters submerged low areas of the delta surface, tidal marshes developed on top of the delta deposits. (Courtesy of the US Geological Survey.)

Glacial delta deposits underlie the Dowds and future Area I Campground and shoreline development. Over many centuries, sound waters helped create the marsh, Tom's Creek, and Dowd's Creek, along with other creeks and estuaries. The delta was the primary focus of development in the 1920s. This aerial view is from 1927. (Courtesy of MHS.)

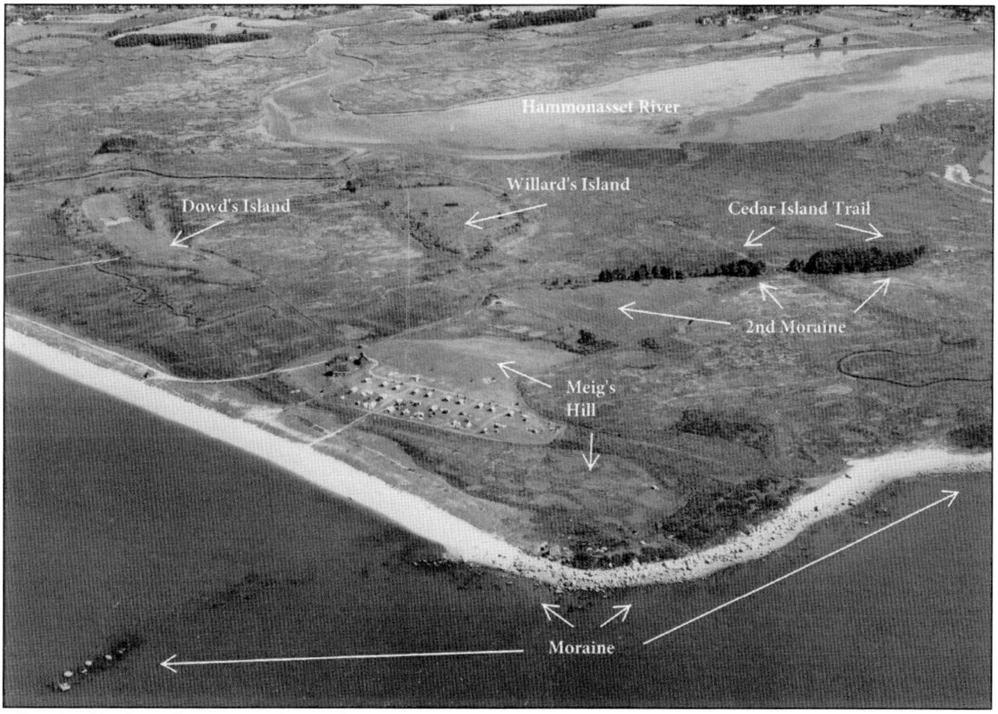

The double lineal moraine formed around 21,000 years ago. The moraines extend quite far offshore and are partially submerged by the sound and Clinton Harbor. Glacial till (unsorted sediment deposits) formed Dowd's, Willard's, and Meigs Island, seen in this 1927 aerial view, but they are not moraines. (Courtesy of MHS.)

This 1927 aerial view shows the Dardanells and Sandy Point Island (note there are no mosquito ditches on the island). Period maps showing a stage coach route across Sandy Point Island are questionable, given the consistently changing marsh and sandy terrain. The Clinton Harbor and Indian River were an important trade center with routes to Europe and the West Indies. (Courtesy of MHS.)

This aerial view shows the remnants of a fishing weir constructed by Native Americans. They used the natural moraine on the upper right, placed the rocks on the left, and caught fish swimming counterclockwise in the Clinton Harbor during high tide. They blocked off the opening as the tide receded, trapping the fish in the weir. (Courtesy of Brian Noe; Keith Hall, pilot.)

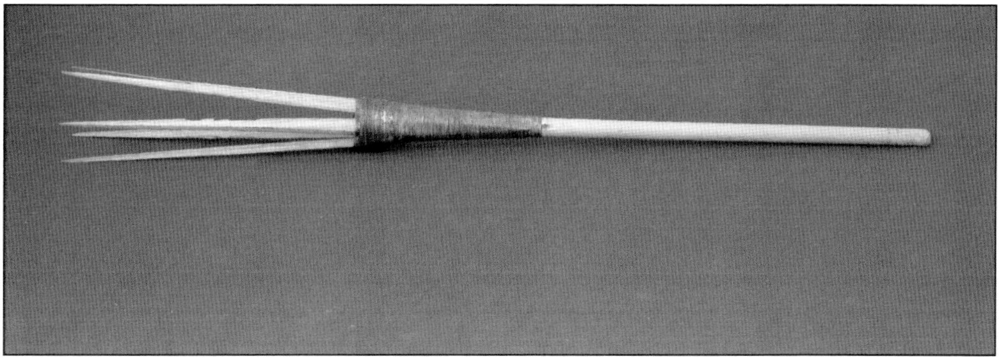

This is a replica made by Gary Nolf of a Native American fishing spear. Designed to be portable and lightweight, this handheld wooden-pronged spear would have been used to catch fish in the man-made weir. (Courtesy of Gary Nolf.)

This is a replica made by Gary Nolf of a Native American basket trap used to catch fish. The trap is woven from sticks and twine into a long cone shape at one end. At the other end of the woven funnel is a hole into which fish swim with no way to escape. (Courtesy of Gary Nolf.)

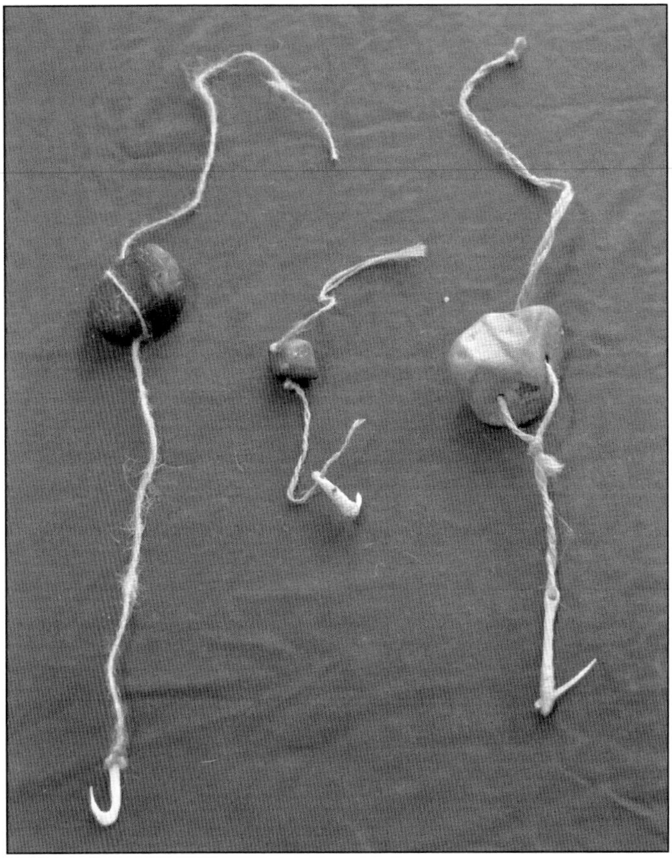

These are examples of bound sinkers (fishing weights) made by Gary Nolf. Native Americans made sinkers of rounded stone tied to a fishing line to drop baited carved-bone hooks to catch bottom-feeding fish. Similar sinkers have been found on Meigs Point. (Courtesy of Gary Nolf.)

This sketch shows a Native American holding an atlatl, or spear-thrower. Launching the spear from the atlatl, the hunter is able to use leverage to maximize velocity and minimize energy during the throw. (Courtesy of the US Forest Service.)

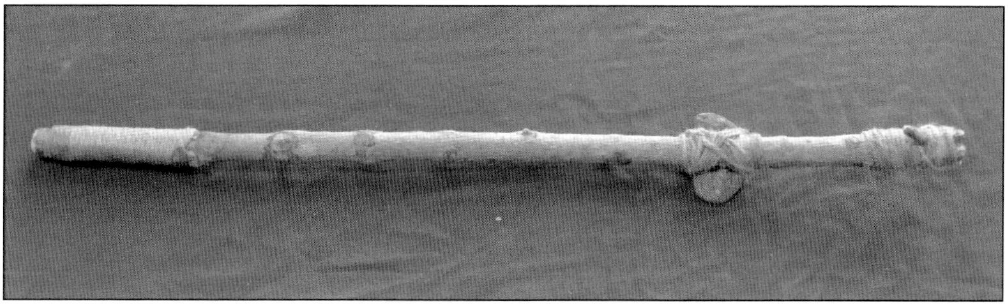

The atlatl was used by Native Americans to generate velocity when launching spears at game animals starting around 10,000 years ago. Archeologists have uncovered use of the atlatl throughout the world. The bow and arrow was not used by Native Americans until around 1,500 years ago. This replica was made by Gary Nolf. (Courtesy of Gary Nolf.)

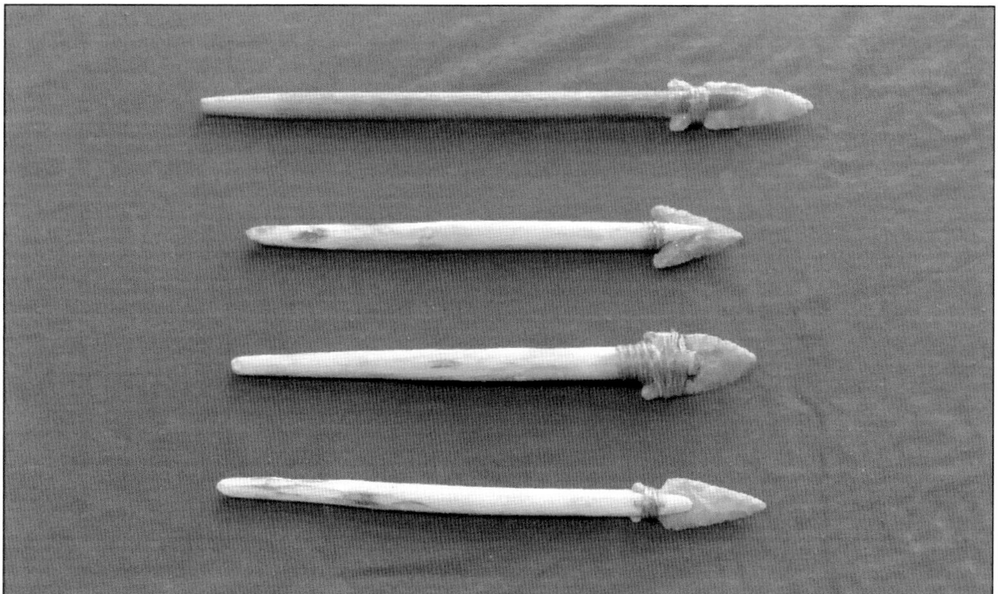

These are four examples of spear tips that fit into the end of the long shaft launched from the atlatl when hunting for game. Native Americans would carry a pouch of these spears with sharp points for efficient hunting. These replicas were made by Gary Nolf. (Courtesy of Gary Nolf.)

Gary Nolf holds a replica he made of a spear shaft used by Native Americans. The fish spear is on top, the game spear is in the middle, and the atlatl is at bottom. Note that the spear tips and shaft were designed to fall out of the spear after striking the target. That allowed the hunter to pick up the spear and reload for another shot without making and carrying an excessive number of spears. (Courtesy of Gary Nolf.)

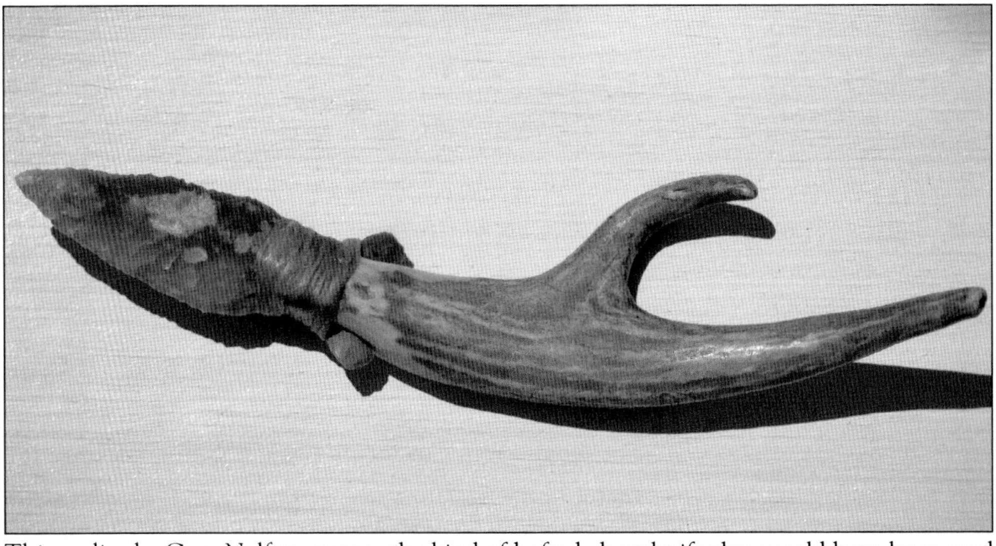

This replica by Gary Nolf represents the kind of hafted chert knife that would have been used by Native Americans. Flint or chert (dark opaque rock composed of silica with a fine-grained texture) points were made from material brought into Connecticut from New York on foot. The haft or handle is made from antler. (Courtesy of Gary Nolf.)

Historic quartz scrapers, discovered at Hammonasset by Don Rankin, were used for scraping and cleaning deer hide and for a variety of cutting purposes. Abundant quartz was the commonly used lithic (stone) material for projectile points and scrapers. Flaking or chipping created the conchoidal cutting edge of these tools. A deer antler was used to make the final sharp edge. (Courtesy of Don Rankin.)

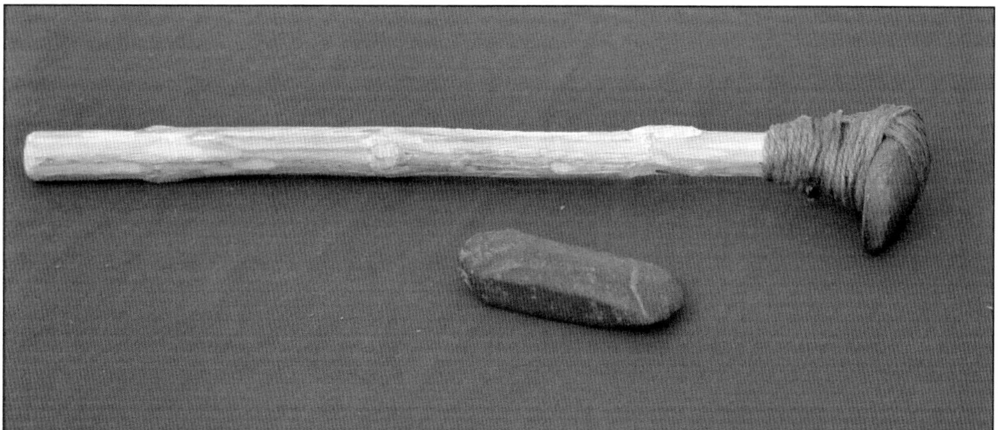

This is a replica made by Gary Nolf of a Native American tool used to dig out canoes and fell trees. The Native Americans would burn the wood of a large log, chipping out the coals. Repeating this process over time, they hollowed out the log and formed it into a canoe. (Courtesy of Gary Nolf.)

This is an excellent example of a stone axe head made of basalt. It is made through pecking at the surface with another stone, then grinding and polishing with sandstone, using water as a lubricant. The blunt end was used as a hammer and the blade end for cutting or splitting wood. (Courtesy of Don Rankin.)

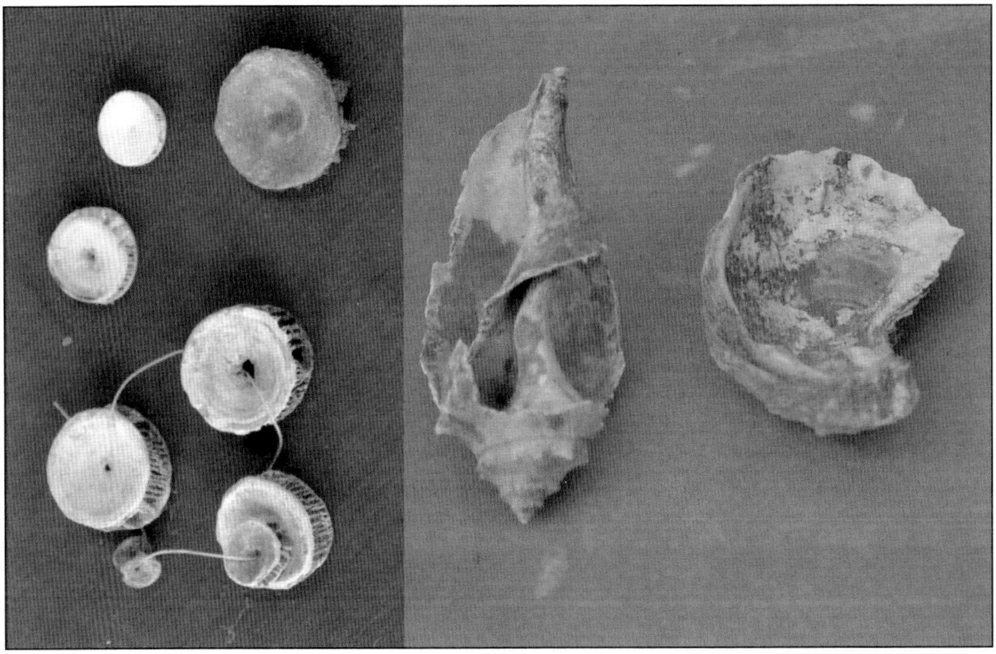

These sea shells from 500 to 1,000 years ago, excavated from a shell midden (a man-made mound of shells) in Westbrook indicate that part of the Native American diet was provided by the mollusks of Long Island Sound, along with fish. The fish vertebrae show that Native Americans were able to capture fairly large fish. (Courtesy of Gary Nolf.)

This shell tempered pot (clay held by broken shells) is an example of Late Woodland Native American pottery dating to 500 to 700 years ago, found in Westport, not far from Hammonasset. This pot would not be placed directly in a fire, but rather in a shallow hole. Rocks from a fire would be placed in water inside this pot to boil water. It was common to drill holes into broken pot pieces and tie the pieces together to make a pot for storing dry goods. (Courtesy of Gary Nolf.)

There were numerous spellings and names for what is now known as Hammonasset. This plate commemorating the Clinton Tercentenary shows one such spelling. The use of the word "plantation" does not indicate that slavery was practiced in the area. The word was commonly used in the 17th century for a site of colonization used to spread Western culture and Christianity. (Courtesy of Gina Woodbury.)

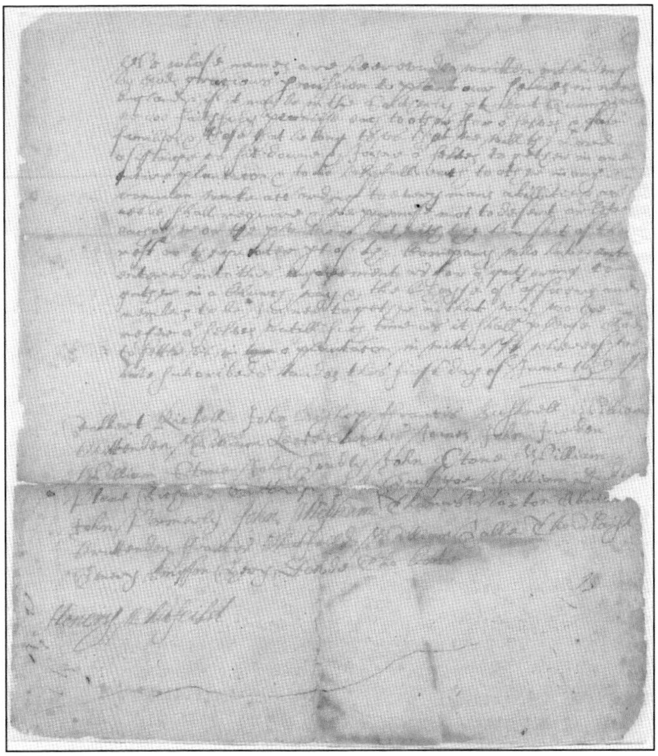

The original Guilford Covenant, binding settlers to remain together on the plantation, was dated June 1, 1639, and read in part, "intending by God's gracious permission to plant ourselves in New England . . . in the southerly part about Quinnipiack . . . join ourselves in one entire plantation." (Courtesy of Massachusetts Historical Society Collections.)

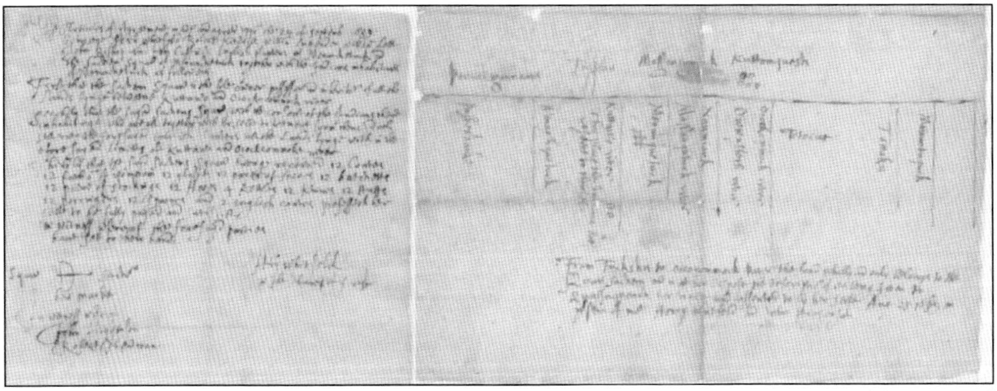

It was unusual for the English settlers to purchase native lands. This image is a copy of the original deed (left) and map (right) of the Guilford Purchase, dated September 29, 1639. The straight line shows the shoreline, and perpendicular lines represent rivers and streams. The rivers and streams are titled by Native American names and clearly define the territory. The Native American names above the shoreline are islands; Massancummock is Faulkner's Island. Rev. Henry Whitfield and associates purchased the land from Sachem squaw Shaumpishuh of the Menuncatuck people, who lived in the Guilford area. Her signature is the large D with what may be an arrow through it. (Courtesy of Massachusetts Historical Society Collections.)

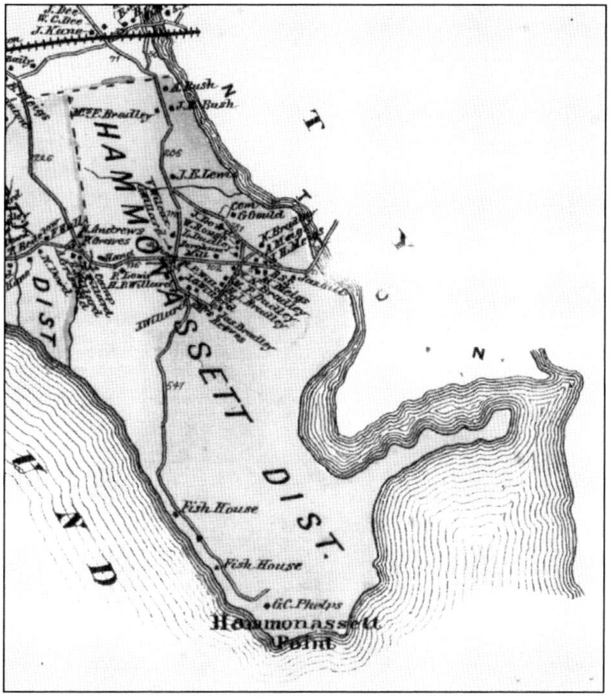

This 1868 map shows the Hammonassett District, which was known as the Hammonassett Quarter until the early 1800s, when the Town of Madison set up school districts. The fish houses on the way to Hammonassett Point (Meigs Point today) processed porpoises for their oil, with the remains used as fertilizer. The farmhouse on Meigs Point was owned by G.C. Phelps. (Courtesy of the Guilford Free Library Historic Room.)

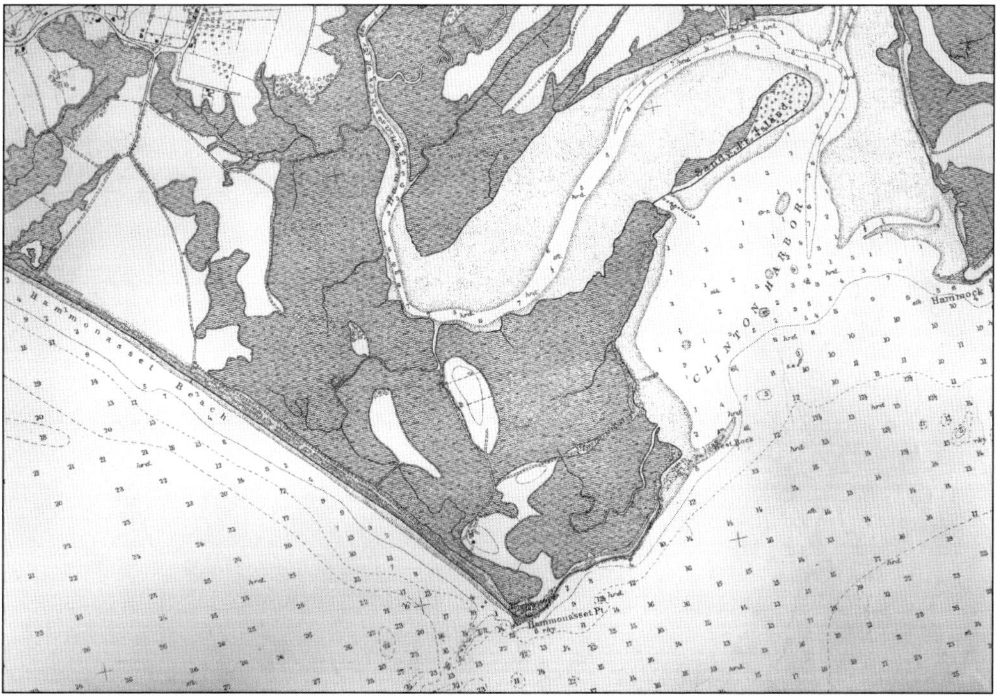

This 1895 Coast and Geodetic Survey map, reissued by the US Geological Survey (USGS) in 1906, is perhaps the first map with a comprehensive survey of Hammonasset Beach. This may also be the first "official" spelling of Hammonasset with one T. The map includes land features and water depth. The USGS survey marker at Hammonasset Point was initially surveyed in 1882 and is relatively easy to find today. (Courtesy of CLEMA.)

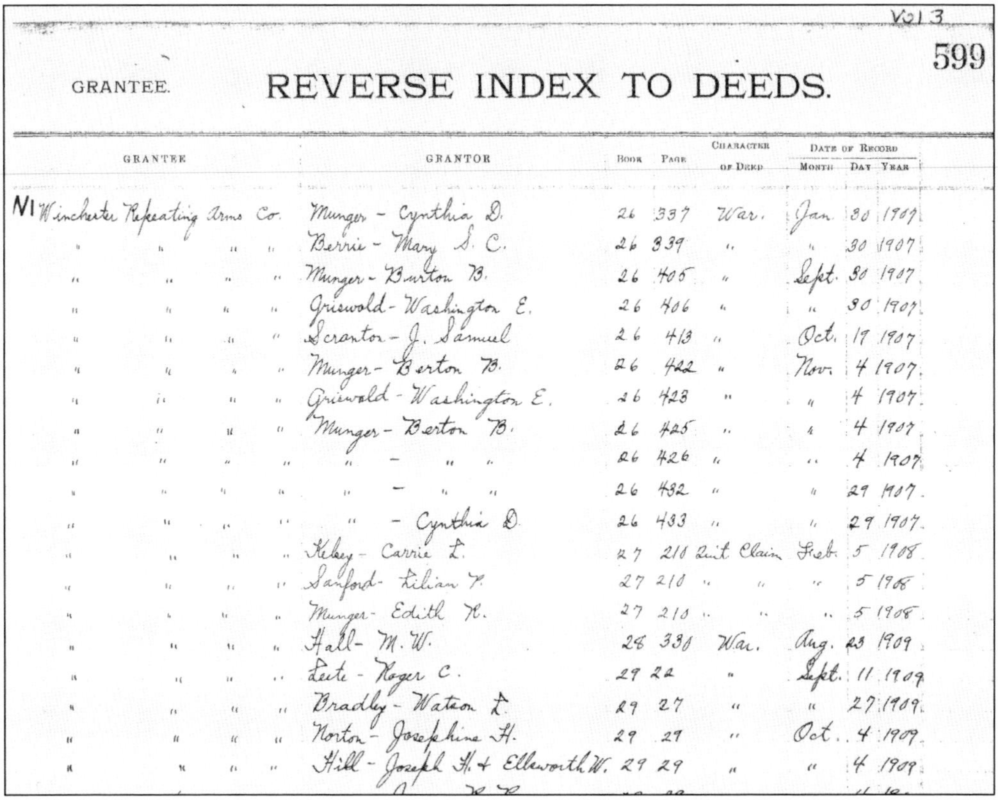

Vol 3

599

GRANTEE. REVERSE INDEX TO DEEDS.

Grantee	Grantor	Book	Page	Character of Deed	Month	Day	Year
N1 Winchester Repeating Arms Co.	Munger - Cynthia D.	26	337	War.	Jan.	30	1907
"	Berrie - Mary S. C.	26	339	"	"	30	1907
"	Munger - Burton B.	26	405	"	Sept.	30	1907
"	Griswold - Washington E.	26	406	"	"	30	1907
"	Scranton - J. Samuel	26	413	"	Oct.	17	1907
"	Munger - Burton B.	26	422	"	Nov.	4	1907
"	Griswold - Washington E.	26	423	"	"	4	1907
"	Munger - Burton B.	26	425	"	"	4	1907
"	" - " "	26	426	"	"	4	1907
"	" - " "	26	432	"	"	29	1907
"	" - Cynthia D.	26	433	"	"	29	1907
"	Kelsey - Carrie L.	27	210	Quit Claim	Feb.	5	1908
"	Sanford - Lilian F.	27	210	"	"	5	1908
"	Munger - Edith R.	27	210	"	"	5	1908
"	Hall - M. W.	28	330	War.	Aug.	23	1909
"	Leete - Roger C.	29	22	"	Sept.	11	1909
"	Bradley - Watson L.	29	27	"	"	27	1909
"	Norton - Josephine H.	29	27	"	Oct.	4	1909
"	Hill - Joseph H. + Ellsworth W.	29	29	"	"	4	1909

The Winchester Repeating Arms Company (WRA) started purchasing a significant amount of Hammonassett Point property in 1907, as can be seen on this land record. It appears that the first property was purchased by Jane E. Winchester on May 20, 1878. It is unknown if the land purchased by Jane E. Winchester was for WRA. (Courtesy of Madison Land Records.)

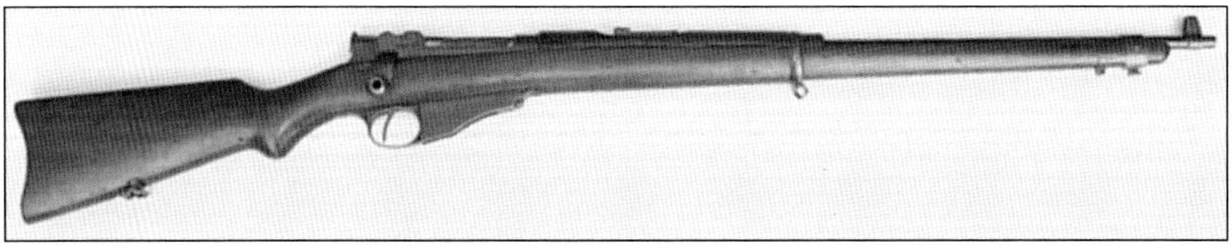

A US Navy contract for the Winchester Lee Rifle, Model 1895, to adopt a modern service rifle to keep pace with other naval powers was the catalyst for the additional investment by WRA at Hammonassett Point. Testing began in 1898, with the decision to develop a permanent rifle range in 1907. Eventually, ordnance was tested here for use in World War I. (Courtesy of Antique Military Rifles.)

WRA used Dowd's Island as a firing range for weapons development. The reinforced road leading to the island indicates heavy use of the site. WRA used the property until 1923, three years after the opening of Hammonassett Beach State Park. (Courtesy of MHS.)

In the 1910s, the WRA erected the target wall seen in the lower right of this 1927 aerial view of Hammonassett Point, called Winchester Point by some (today called Meigs Point), to capture and analyze fired projectiles. The wall also helped to protect watercraft. (Courtesy of MHS.)

This 1937 photograph shows what remained of the WRA test fire wall. The WRA office building at upper right, rebuilt in 1917, was used as the Meigs Point manager's house for decades before becoming the Meigs Point Nature Center in 1972. The building is now used as an auxiliary building to support the new nature center that was dedicated in 2016. (Courtesy of Jeff Barske.)

These rusted metal objects were among the remains found in the sand at the base of the WRA target practice wall built over 100 years ago. The middle object appears to be a bolt, along with pieces of what are probably the original brackets. (Courtesy of Shelby Docker.)

Two

Extraordinary People

Many individuals, including full time and seasonal staff and volunteers, have helped to make Hammonasset Beach State Park the enjoyable, magical place it is today. There are, however, certain extraordinary individuals who deserve special recognition for the leadership they showed in the creation of this park.

The creation of the first State Park Commission and the founding of Hammonasset are remarkable accomplishments. The original six appointed commission members were Chairman Edward Bradley, John Calhoun, Herman Chapman, John Fox, Lucius Robinson, and Edward Wilkins, with state forester Walter Filley, ex-officio. Chairman Bradley and Commissioner Robinson were part of the 1911 Study Commission that influenced the Connecticut General Assembly to create the commission. The first meeting was held on September 29, 1913. In March 1914, Albert Turner, field secretary, became the first employee of the commission.

Dedication was the core of the commissioners: Bradley died in office after serving more than five years. Robinson served over 29 years, Calhoun over 21 years, Chapman over 34 years, Wilkins 28 years, Fayette Wright almost 11 years, Filley over 33 years, and Turner over 27 years. Arthur Parker was the first general park supervisor, a position he held for 28 years. William F. Miller worked at Hammonasset for over 40 years, eventually becoming director of Connecticut State Parks.

The tone and culture set by Chairman Bradley is best exemplified by Turner's words upon Bradley's passing in January 1917: "it is impossible to omit a few words of personal tribute to the character of General Bradley, whose loss we have all felt keenly. His gentle and persistent optimism in the face of every discouragement, his faith in his ideals, his invariable good humor and kindly smile, and that rare courtesy and charm of manner which his friends can never forget; all these traits were his, and the memory of them is ours." Commitment, continuity, and dedication are the qualities that helped make Hammonasset Beach State Park the flagship of the Connecticut state park system.

This October 12, 1914, photograph shows five of the six original commissioners. From left to right are John Calhoun, field secretary Albert Turner, Edward Wilkins, Lucius Robinson, Edward Bradley, and Herman Chapman, believed to be on the Connecticut River on the yacht *Halcyon* with Commodore Russell to inspect land related to the acquisition of Hurd State Park. Commissioner John Fox was not present.

Former Connecticut adjutant general Edward E. Bradley headed an exploratory commission in 1911 that influenced the Connecticut General Assembly to create the State Park Commission in 1913. Bradley was the first chairman. He was a prominent New Haven business leader and legislator and served with the New Haven Grays militia, which fought 20 battles during the Civil War. His sudden passing in January 1917 was felt keenly by all.

Founding commissioner Lucius Franklin Robinson "temporarily" took over as commission chairman in 1917 but ended up serving until 1937. He remained on the commission until his death on June 11, 1941. Commissioner Robinson earned a "get it done" reputation, directly negotiating with landowners to purchase land and if necessary using condemnation (now known as eminent domain) to acquire land. (Courtesy of Robinson & Cole LLP.)

On January 24, 1914, the park commissioners voted Albert Turner as field secretary with a $150 monthly salary. After an extensive survey of the Connecticut coastline, Turner identified five prime beach properties for state park development. Instrumental in park development, Turner would stay on with the park commission until his retirement in 1942. He attended at least 348 commission meetings. He is pictured here in 1935.

Arthur Harris Whittemore Sr. was appointed to the State Park Commission on May 1923 and served until his sudden death on November 29, 1927, at 63. Whittemore was a Naugatuck industrialist whose family business purchased the Winchester Repeating Arms company property in 1923 and leased it to the state until funds were available to purchase the property for Hammonasset in 1925.

This rare group photograph shows the commissioners outside of the Assembly Building on Cedar Knoll on July 8, 1936. A Hammonasset meeting included the traditional swim (including a 1919 "birthday clothes" swim by a few who will remain nameless) and a Clam Shed lunch. From left to right are Commissioners Filley (former state forester), Whittemore Jr. (who replaced his father on the commission), Dwight Wheeler, Robinson, Arthur Peale, Chapman, and Wilkins. The Meigs Cottage and Hills Cottage can be seen at right.

Erastus Hull, seated at the pavilion, worked at Hammonasset making window screens, lattices, and other useful objects, including map cases. He delighted in the changes at the park until his death shortly after being hit by a trolley at around age 90 in 1928. Many park employees lived in state owned housing. Hull lived in the old Arthur Bradley house acquired by the park commission.

Nurses like Nellie Nettleton, Caroline Hawkins, and matron Elsie Woodruff, pictured left to right in the summer of 1936, provided first aid to visitors in the Administration Building, constructed in 1925. A tent was used as a first aid station before 1925. Anywhere from 700 to 1,700 incidents were logged in any given summer, including jellyfish stings, cuts due to broken glass or rocks, and occasional serious injury or illness.

In 1921, the commissioners realized they needed police to keep order. Legislation passed in 1922 allowed the commission to appoint special police. In 1929, at age 37, Homer Miller (pictured) was appointed a park policeman to serve at all parks. A Madison farmer and a field artillery private in World War I, Miller loved to patrol Hammonasset on horseback. Numerous visitors caught changing in cars were ejected with $1 tickets.

This unidentified employee protected valuables for park visitors enjoying the day at Hammonasset. Valuables were stored in a vault behind steel bars in the Grand Pavilion. The sign reads "Call for Valuables Here." Note the white shirt and tie worn during the hot summer months. (Courtesy of CLEMA.)

The Hammonasset Clam Shed served hundreds of thousands per summer season, generating significant revenue. The 1936 crew, as identified by CLEMA, was, from left to right, Lucy McCamm, Alan Miller, Lucien Christianson, Horan, "Toots" Sullivan, possibly Ed Berger, Sherwood Berger, manager Leo Sullivan, possibly Leistner, unidentified (seated), unidentified, Fred Miller, cashier ? Maloney, and unidentified.

Sherwood Berger takes what appears to be a much needed cigarette break on a hot summer day working at the Clam Shed at Hammonasset. (Courtesy of CLEMA.)

The 1936 Hammonasset Beach State Park office crew was, from left to right, L. Wayne Adams, John Park, Alfred Miller (age 21), Adelbert Cox, and William F. Miller (age 16). Al and Bill Miller were born in 1920 and 1915 respectively on land owned by their father, Joseph Miller, that was later purchased for Hammonasset. Both worked at the park in various capacities for decades. (Courtesy of CLEMA.)

This photograph, taken sometime after 1935, shows members of the Hammonasset winter work crew, probably at the Duck Hole Road facility, which supported all the state parks. From left to right are supervisor of construction Frank Sellew, R. Killz, possibly Alfred Miller, the six-foot-one William Miller, and Lloyd Huested. The park was in a constant state of improvement, and existing buildings required year-round maintenance, weather permitting.

William F. Miller sold milk to vendors, pushed hot dogs at the Clam Shed at 15, was a lifeguard during college, served in the Army Air Corps in the Pacific, and then returned to work for the State Park and Forest Commission, becoming director of state parks in 1971. After 40 years of service, he was memorialized with the William F. Miller Campground.

Hammonasset Beach State Park hired lifeguards every summer season. The 17-man 1936 crew is seen here in a rowboat used to patrol the waters and rescue swimmers in distress. The lifeguards rescued 20 to 40 swimmers during a summer season.

This 1941 photograph was taken in the refectory (cafeteria) in the Clam Shed. J. Valenti is behind the counter, while police officers George DeVoe (left) and Tom Kelly ham it up for the camera. According to the park commission minutes, the first park arrest was made in July 1927 "all on account of good, or bad, liquor," during Prohibition. The first police vehicle was purchased in 1930 for $1,000. Counter window closures protected equipment and supplies.

It was not uncommon for park employees to work, play, and sometimes live in housing at the park. This 1939 photograph shows John Park winding up for a baseball pitch on the beach. Park served the commission faithfully starting in 1922 and eventually earned the title of superintendent.

Three

We Buy Land and Move Houses

Starting in 1919, land and building acquisition was both swift and determined. In the 1920s, the meaning of *Hammonasset*, "where we dig holes in the ground," could have been changed to "we buy land and move houses." Due to the lack of support for state parks in the Connecticut General Assembly and competing demands to support World War I, it took six years before the State Park Commission finally had a budget to start purchasing land to create Hammonasset. From 1913 until 1918, million-dollar budget requests were met with $20,000 appropriations.

Pressure mounted as the five locations identified by field secretary Albert Turner as potential shorefront state park sites were quickly being lost to private development. The commissioners started using the code name "shore park" in meeting minutes to try and protect the identity of their prized shoreline property from private developers.

One possible reason for Hammonasset being left intact and available for purchase was the vicious marsh mosquitoes and green flies. Hammonasset Point (Meigs Point today) was known as Mosquito Point by locals. Or perhaps the land was available because people didn't want the WRA rifle testing range as a neighbor. Some homeowners, in direct negotiations with the commissioners, readily sold their properties. Some property owners sold their land and became enthusiastic supporters, and a few even became park employees.

Those unwilling to sell would likely end up meeting Chairman Lucius Robinson in person, reluctantly selling or facing condemnation. When contested, the courts awarded all properties to the commission, sometimes at a higher price than originally offered, sometimes lower.

It was not uncommon for park employees to live in the houses that came with the land purchased for the park. Many houses were moved around the park and repurposed for manager housing or administrative offices. Materials from the houses and buildings that were razed were used to build or repair other structures.

There are a few structures remaining from the original days of Hammonasset development that can be found today. Imagine the life people enjoyed living in these buildings, and then visit those buildings from the 1920s in person.

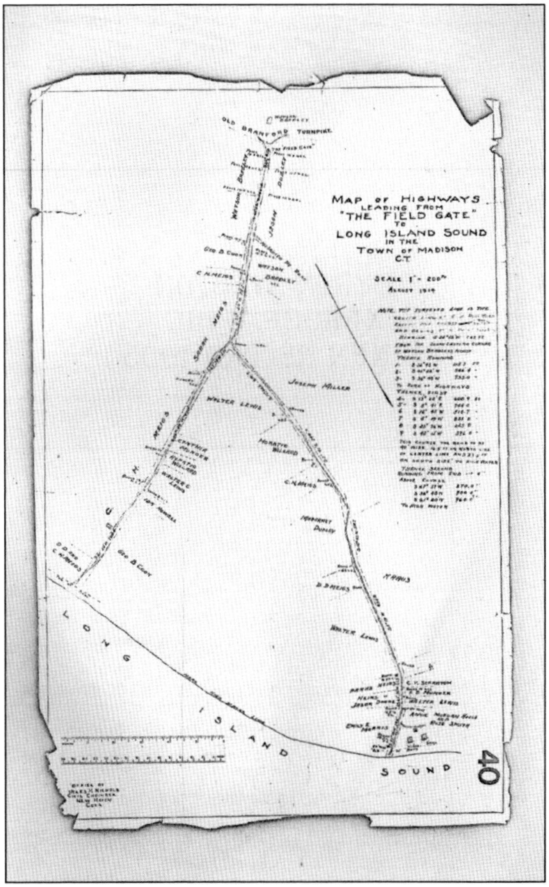

This 1914 map shows the two main roads into Hammonasset and the names of property owners. Note the aptly named Mosquito Point Road near the top of the map. (Courtesy of CLEMA.)

Hammonasset Beach visitors would see this view of the Watson Bradley House when leaving the park, purchased in 1919 for $6,000. The park entrance intersected with the Old Branford Turnpike, not Boston Post Road, which is on the other side of these properties. This 1925 view shows trolley tracks on the right (running northeast to southwest) used by the New Haven & Shore Line Trolley Seabreeze Route into Hammonasset from 1924 to 1927.

Visitors and campers driving into Hammonasset would pass the Cusano house on their left not far from the Watson Bradley House. The sign hanging on the side of the porch reads "Homemade Kreeme Fudge." Cream is the yellowish fatty component of non-homogenized milk that tends to accumulate at the surface. Note the trolley tracks on a bed of sand. Trolley travel was a precarious venture.

This 1927 aerial view shows the entrance to Hammonasset off of Old Branford Turnpike. The Cusano family offered their land and house (right) for $5,000 shortly after trolley tracks were installed in 1924. Lack of funds delayed the transaction until 1928, when it was completed via condemnation for $4,000, double the commission offer of $2,000. There are no entrance booths here, as entry to the park was free. (Courtesy of MHS.)

This 1925 photograph shows the Cooke house, one of the first properties acquired in August 1919 by C.A. Ferry, an agent of the commission. The acquisition included 145 acres (Area I Camp) with buildings for $15,000. The main house, on the north side of Route 1, was rented and the income used to pay park expenses. The house, now privately owned, still stands in its original location.

The Horatio Willard House (left) and Willard Cottage (right), shown in 1925, were acquired in August 1919 with 36 acres and buildings for $8,010. It is believed that the house was in the vicinity of the Old Branford Turnpike. The cottage sat on the southern side of the Boston Post Road and west side of the Old Branford Turnpike (seen in the photograph). The house survived the 1938 hurricane.

Another August 1919 purchase included a 23-acre portion of the Dudley farm with buildings, acquired for $4,200. The property bordered the eastern side of the main entrance. The Dudley home, shown here in 1925, still stands today.

The Arthur J. Bradley house, purchased in 1919 or 1920 for an unknown sum, was occupied by park employee Erastus Hull. Arthur Bradley (no relation to commission chairman Edward Bradley) agreed to maintain the house, but the repairs became unduly burdensome by 1921. The park stepped in to ensure Hull's occupancy.

This 1925 photograph taken from the beach shows the WRA buildings and land sold in 1923 to the J.H. Whittemore Company. Commissioner Harris Whittemore Sr. was the family owner of the company. The company leased the land to the state for $1 per year. Note that there are two barns to the left of the office, several outbuildings, and poles that previously held telegraph lines.

The J.H. Whittemore Company sold the WRA property purchased in 1923 to the state for $55,000 in 1925. WRA rebuilt the house in the late 1910s. It is in use today next to the new Meigs Point Nature Center, dedicated in 2016. Dowd's Island (upper left) and Willard's Island (top center) were included in the purchase. (Courtesy of MHS.)

This 1925 photograph shows the Pittard House and property, which served as a home for Mr. George Norman Pittard, superintendent of grounds, who was responsible for "everything," according to the commission reports. The house and land were in the northeastern section of the park, where offices and maintenance buildings are today.

This September 1938 aerial view, taken after the hurricane, shows the Pittard House and property at lower left, with the maintenance building built in 1929 above it. The Dudley house is at bottom right. The two-lane Dowd's Point Road heading out to Dowd's Point is now called Beach Road. (Courtesy of the State of Connecticut Public Library.)

Clarkson Meigs, representing both himself and his brother D.D. Meigs, rather reluctantly tendered some 50 acres with one house, pictured in 1925, and about 1,400 feet of shore frontage, including Dowd's Point shoreline (Beach Road), for $25,125, as noted in commission minutes of August 11, 1919. The 1921 Chevy next to the cottage was advertised for $680. Note Tom's Hill/Dowd's Camp Ground in the background.

Alice B. White sold her house (center, on the beach) in 1925 with 100 feet of frontage and three acres of salt meadow for $3,500. T.A. Stewart offered his house (right, on the beach) for $5,000 via letter in June 1925, but state funds were not available. Helen Horton Stewart (Mrs. Thomas A. Stewart) agreed to sell the house and her 50-by-100-foot lot for $2,500 in October 1925. (Courtesy of MHS.)

The Harlow, Smith, and Hills Cottages are pictured in 1927. The Harlow and Smith properties were awarded by condemnation in February 1928 for $10,317 (the commission offered $6,000; Harlow asked $15,000). The Smith property was awarded for $17,368 (the commission offered $13,000; Smith asked $16,500). The Hills house was leased by the commission until purchased in August 1927 for $12,000. Note the concrete retaining walls. (Courtesy of MHS.)

This 1927 aerial view shows desirable land the commission competed for against private developers. Purchases in the 1920s and 1930s were by agreement, sometimes reluctantly after landowners were threatened with condemnation. In the 1930s, most acquisitions consisted of small marsh and upland parcels. In 1931, a significant portion of Great Major Island was purchased from Mr. Coe along with other land for $325. (Courtesy of MHS.)

In 1928, the C.H. Meigs Cottage is being moved to the newly named Cedar Knoll at a cost of $1,500. A Fordson tractor (produced by Henry Ford and Son) provided the pulling power. The Grand Pavilion is in the background. Cedar Knoll was developed as an administration complex.

The Meigs Cottage can be seen at upper left on its way to Cedar Knoll. This 1928 photograph taken from the newly erected bathhouse deck shows the free short-term camp, walkways and ramps over the dunes, and the Harlow and Smith Cottages (the Hills Cottage is obscured) on the beachfront at right. Meigs Point buildings can be seen in the background.

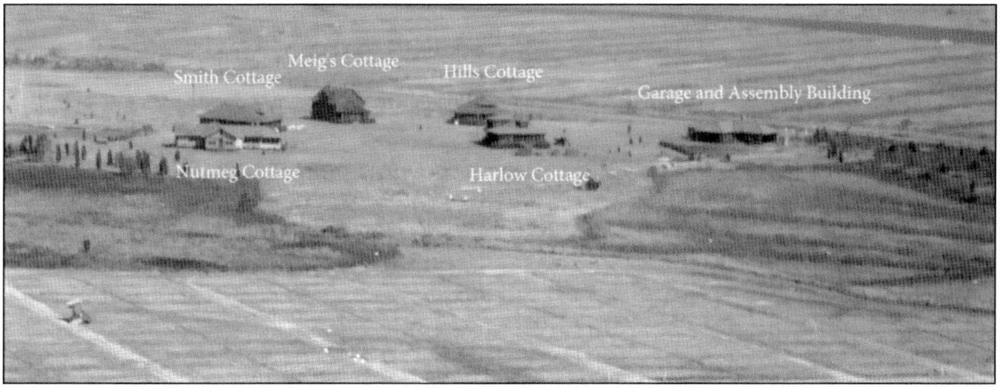

The Meigs Cottage was joined on Cedar Knoll by the Harlow, Smith, and Hills Cottages, moved in 1930 for $5,000. The Nutmeg Cottage was built in 1931 to feed 50 employees and house lifeguards and staff. The garage and assembly building was built in 1934. The marshland (right and below Assembly Building) was sold for $350 by Flora M. Dailey of Plymouth, Connecticut, in 1943.

This 1930 photograph shows the Hills Cottage fireplace, left behind when the cottage was moved to Cedar Knoll. A sidewalk to the porch can be seen at right. In center in the distance appears to be equipment cleaning up the recently moved or razed Alice B. White or T.A. Stewart Cottage.

The Joseph and Marie Miller house (also the home of Alfred and William Miller) was purchased for $13,500 by the state highway commission in 1936 to make way for the new Hammonasset Park entrance. The Millers were provided life tenure in a suitable building within the park. This was one of the few recorded significant land acquisitions in the 1930s, due to budget constraints during the Depression. (Courtesy of MHS.)

The Cusano house was moved in 1940 or 1941 from the main entrance road to the top of Tom's Hill and tucked into the trees at the end of what is now P Street overlooking Dowd's Camp. This 1941 photograph shows upgraded camping facilities, an extension of today's O Street, and the new field circle with flagpole. The house was used by the camp inspector.

Four

If We Build It, Will They Come?

How were the state park commissioners able to determine where and what to build with just a field engineer, no marketing department, a skeptical general public, and a hostile general assembly? The commissioners recognized that "neither the General Assembly nor the public has followed us fully in our growth toward a due conception of the State Park problem. We must, therefore, make some of our acquisitions available for public use at once, in order to demonstrate the practicability of our plans." Congestion problems in the 1910s at Savin Rock State Park in West Haven, Connecticut, adversely affected the commission's reputation and ability to obtain funding to build out the state park system. The answer as to why the commission built structures over and around susceptible marshes and creeks will be revealed in this chapter.

The commission learned from the Savin Rock congestion problems and would not repeat those mistakes at Hammonasset. Plans included building a broad, impressive boulevard, water and sanitation, a restaurant, bathhouses, campsites, and open spaces for aviation and field sports; eliminating mosquitoes through ditch draining, and giving "the most careful attention that the natural beauty . . . remain unimpaired."

The breathtaking speed of construction simply could not be matched in today's era of extensive planning and permitting. Plans were developed, materials secured, and structures completed in a matter of months. The commission made Hammonasset the flagship of the state park system. No reasonable obstacle could stop it, although the lack of funds curtailed the commission's dreams and vision of a grand resort that included colonnades, boulevards, pavilions, spires, and the best amenities. Explosive attendance at Hammonasset thrilled the commissioners, who responded by building out the park.

Although the commissioners believed that the state parks should operate on user fees, which worked until the Depression, Hammonasset was not able to generate the revenue to acquire land and build structures and infrastructure from these fees alone. Reliance on the general assembly for acquisition and development funding, with no support for a bond program, frustrated the commissioners and greatly hampered the development of Hammonasset and other state parks.

This 1919 rendering depicts the "Bathing Pavilion and Head House—Hammonasset Beach Park—Madison Conn." A head house is an enclosed building with lockers and a bathhouse attached to an open-sided shed with pavilion seating. As with most of the proposed plans for Hammonasset development, a lack of funding meant eliminating features such as the twin spires and flags.

The completed Grand Pavilion is seen on August 3, 1920, from the water. The pavilion was constructed in approximately eight months. The Grand Pavilion remained into the 1960s, surviving the elements, hurricanes, and millions of happy visitors.

The state park commissioners' priority was the hard working citizenry of Connecticut. The commissioners recognized the need for public access to Long Island Sound, which was becoming privatized, developed, and cut off from the public at an alarming rate. Connecticut's working class, mainly immigrants, needed and deserved an escape from six-day work weeks and crowded cities. Here, Union Manufacturing Foundry Department workers in New Britain pose on November 8, 1911. (Courtesy of the New Britain Public Library Local History Room Collection.)

The utility and work rooms take shape, with the pylons for the women's bathhouse in place (left) and framing for the men's bathhouse underway at right.

The men's bathhouse floor is done, with lumber ready to complete the project.

The women's bathhouse is under construction, with lumber and posts ready to go. The C.H. Meigs Cottage, recently purchased by the park commission, is in the background.

The women's bathhouse roof is starting to take shape, along with the laundry building. The structure seems a bit tilted.

The final product can be visualized with the men's bathhouse near completion and the Grand Pavilion area roofed but with no walls.

Two workers build the boardwalk ramp connecting the men's bathhouse with the nearly complete utility room. The wall is not yet affixed on the men's bathhouse. The photographer is facing west, toward Webster Point.

The ramp on the west (Tom's Creek) side of the Grand Pavilion was the main access to this grand structure. Walls, stairs, and railings are waiting to be done.

The interior of the Grand Pavilion is ready for picnic tables, benches, and visitors in 1920.

People enjoy a tour of the nearly completed Grand Pavilion on August 3, 1920. Note that there are no colonnades or benches, and many other buildings and conveniences are waiting to be developed. The Harlow, Smith, and Hills Cottages can be seen in the background, with a flag waving in the sea breeze. The still-used WRA target wall can be seen on Winchester Point (formerly Hammonasset Point, informally Mosquito Point, and currently Meigs Point).

A couple takes a leisurely walk back to their car after touring the Grand Pavilion and beach. Note that railings and other finishing touches are still in progress. Given the attire of the couple, perhaps it was a cool August day at the shoreline.

The separate entrance to the women's bathhouse ran under the pavilion to the right of the main stairway to the beach. The entrance to the men's bathhouse was on the left. However, there was only one locker attendant, so men and women mixed in the area outside the locker rooms, not an optimal situation. This problem would be corrected later.

This photograph, believed to be from late summer 1920, captures the magnificence of the Grand Pavilion. The main entrance to the pavilion from the parking lot is on the left, the men's bathhouse entrance is under the pavilion, and the main stairs to the beach are on the right.

This 1921 photograph shows the popularity of the Grand Pavilion at Hammonasset Beach. Many people brought picnic lunches to enjoy in the pavilion. Expansion was already underway in 1921 with the construction of the Clam Shed and colonnade. The colonnade would quickly become known as the boardwalk. Major building development continued through 1928.

This view of the beach from the vicinity of the Grand Pavilion faces west toward Tom's Creek and Webster Point in Madison. Note the tent pitched for the day and the people in suits and dresses.

Undeveloped Hammonasset Beach is pictured in 1920. The privately owned Smith, Hills, and Harlow Cottages can be seen in the background of this picture, taken from the vicinity of the Grand Pavilion facing east towards Winchester (Meigs) Point.

The overwhelming popularity of Hammonasset Beach State Park led to construction of the Clam Shed for serving food and beverages to visitors. This photograph shows the uncompleted Clam Shed serving people in September 1921. The chimney is not yet finished. Note the wheel under the Clam Shed that may have been used to open and close a water valve.

This 1922 photograph shows the Clam Shed with completed chimney, kiosks, and stairs to the beach. The free short-term (weekends only) camps can be seen on the left. Note the marsh between the Grand Pavilion and Clam Shed.

This view of the grand boulevard was taken from the roof of the Grand Pavilion on a late summer day in 1920. Beginning with the 1921 summer season, Hammonasset would be overwhelmed with visitors and campers as word of the beautiful new state park spread. The C.H. Meigs Cottage is on the left.

This 1921 photograph shows the newly completed boardwalk and stairs to the Clam Shed. The multiple levels of the Grand Pavilion can be seen. Food service and picnicking is on the top floor. The second floor is the walkway to the women's bathhouse. Note the elevation of the functional space, built over marsh, to help protect the building from floods. This was done on all buildings and the boardwalk.

This September 4, 1921, photograph was taken from the ramp and stairs to the beach in front of the Clam Shed. Park staff was consistently challenged to keep people off the fragile dunes. The spongy sand of Hammonasset compacts when walked on, making it very difficult for dune grass to thrive and protect the beach from storms and tides.

Entering the 1924 summer season, ingenious Hammonasset staff built benches to provide people a place to sit and help protect the dunes. A fence was added along the boardwalk support pylons to complete protection of the dunes. The boardwalk railing brackets were a tripping hazard, so the park rebuilt the railings, converting the brackets into support for boardwalk benches. A lifeguard tower was also added to help protect swimmers.

Two canvas tents were added in 1923 that housed the lifeguard and first aid staff. The tents were also used by the night watchmen.

This May 1926 photograph from the water shows, from left to right, the C.H. Meigs Cottage, the Grand Pavilion, the new Administrative Building constructed in 1925, and the Clam Shed.

Park officials were concerned that tides would choke off Tom's Creek from the sound. The creek is thought to be named after Thomas Dowd, who owned property on Webster's Point. It is believed that Dowd's Creek was naturally choked off from the sound in the 1890s. Louis H. Hall of Madison agreed to pay half of the cost of a bulkhead. (Courtesy of MHS.)

The first known bulkhead was built in 1926. Comparing these 1927 aerial photographs, the mouth of Tom's Creek continued to change wildly despite construction of the dual bulkheads. The bulkheads were wiped out during the 1938 hurricane, creating issues for decades for Hammonasset and the private property owners on Webster's Point in Madison. (Courtesy of MHS.)

Beachfront development of Hammonasset is seen in 1927. The commissioners continued to endure some public criticism of state parks as a waste of taxpayer money as well as legislative reluctance to provide funding for future development and acquisition of additional land for Hammonasset and to create other state parks. They needed to quickly build out Hammonasset as the flagship park to promote and advertise success to a still skeptical public and to lobby for a larger budget. Some locals criticized building over marsh and Dowd's Creek, but the commission did not own any other suitable beachfront to develop until 1930. In addition, part of the road from the paid parking lot to Meigs Point was privately owned and barely adequate for light traffic. The commission paid a lease fee to the private landowners for use of the road. (Courtesy of MHS.)

New bathhouses were constructed in 1928 (top) to accommodate the high demand for facilities. The space between the bathhouses and boardwalk was reserved to construct a pavilion for food service and picnic tables to match the Grand Pavilion. The budget was $77,000 but was cancelled due to the Depression. The short-term camps were expanded and moved to the other side of Dowd's Creek to make way for the new bathhouses. The paid parking lot was eliminated. The Smith, Hills, and Harlow Cottages were moved in 1930. The 1929 kitchen expansion at the Clam Shed can be seen with four new vents and a reconfigured flat roof. The main stairs of the Grand Pavilion have been replaced by a boardwalk and ramps. The boardwalk was extended past the Grand Pavilion towards the Dowd's (Camper's) Beach between 1928 and 1930 (bottom).

This is the only known photograph of a trolley car running in Hammonasset. The trolley ran from 1924 through 1927. The Hammonasset spur was part of the New Haven & Shore Line Railway Company Seabreeze Route between Guilford and Old Saybrook. The trip from Foxon Park in New Haven to Hammonasset was 15.98 miles and took 1 hour and 22 minutes. (Courtesy of MHS.)

This picture shows a New Haven & Shore Line Railway trolley making a run down Route 1 in Madison. The Sperry Engineering Company of New Haven, builders of the Shore Line, took over the line from New Haven to Old Saybrook on July 17, 1923, to consolidate operations as the New Haven & Shore Line and stave off bankruptcy. (Courtesy of CLEMA.)

This is the "Hammonasset Car." It is believed that during the busy summer season a sign was placed on random cars running to Hammonasset. The New Haven & Shore Line Railway Co. was constantly staving off bankruptcy, which meant minimal maintenance on the cars. The company also requested subsidies from the park commission, which were considered but denied. (Courtesy of CLEMA.)

Trolley travel was precarious; there were numerous accidents with other vehicles, horse-pulled wagons, and people. This 1920 photograph shows a trolley derailment in Madison, apparently not an uncommon occurrence. There were two head-on collisions in other towns in 1917 and 1919, killing many and injuring more. Poor finances led to strikes in 1919, forcing the company to hire strikebreakers. (Courtesy of CLEMA.)

The stairs on the Grand Pavilion (above) were in need of repair for the 1928 season. Park staff replaced the stairs with a center ramp to the Grand Pavilion (below) and extended the boardwalk 16 feet west of the structure to connect a ramp to the parking area. This reduced the pedestrian traffic through the pavilion and made is easier for people with walking limitations to enjoy the park.

In 1925, Hammonasset retired its old small REO Speed Wagon, purchasing a new two-and-a-half-ton REO Speed Wagon for general work at all the parks. REO stands for Ransom Eli Olds, known as one of the better manufacturers of commercial vehicles. R.E. Olds was also known for Oldsmobile. (Courtesy of Myn Transport Blog.)

The L-shaped storage building completed in 1930 can be seen to the right of the main entrance and field circle built to help control traffic. Park employees built the facility with leftover supplies for a total cost of only $400. The facility supported all state parks, which was problematic due to inadequate space. A new site was selected on Duck Hole Road to support all state parks. This photograph was taken in 1938.

This foggy-day photograph, taken sometime in 1932, shows the bathhouses and new short-term camp area. Faucets were added for daily visitors and campers. A temporary walkway was installed to help people walk more easily and protect the dunes. Park employees planted poison ivy to further help protect the dunes.

In 1928, the Meigs Point Road was one lane with minimal infrastructure. There were no walkways and only a handful of ramps to get to the beach. Outhouses and changing stations were infrequent. Outhouses were sometimes referred to as "Chic Sales" after a popular vaudeville comedian of the 1920s and 1930s.

In 1931, park staff constructed a new six-foot walkway of gravel and cinder with ramps from the street to the beach around 500 feet apart from the Clam Shed to Meigs Point. Telephone cables were put underground to reduce cost for $850. Over 4,000 feet of chestnut-pole curbing six to eight inches square provided spaces for 455 cars to nose into at a 45-degree angle. Additional Chic Sales were needed to meet popular demand. (Courtesy of Jeff Barske.)

Over the winter of 1933–1934, a new two-lane boulevard entrance was constructed with other interior road work. The federal government approved Civil Works Administration Project No. 70, providing 700 men to the 25 state parks. Wages for unskilled labor were $15 per week, and foremen and skilled supervisors were paid $24 to $50 per week. State park employees still on payroll supervised the CWA employees.

In October 1936, the commission approved a new entrance to Hammonasset (seen in this 1938 aerial view) as presented by Charles Taylor of the State Highway Department despite the opposition of field secretary Albert Turner and superintendent Arthur V. Parker. The open field to the left of the Cook house (top center) is the Area I Camps today. (Courtesy of the State of Connecticut Public Library.)

In 1940, posts were driven to build an eight-foot-wide boardwalk to Tom's Creek. Although unlikely, it is not known if the boardwalk was completed past the Dowd's Road campsites. These posts, exposed at low tide near Tom's Creek, may be their remains. If true, this illustrates the severe beach erosion over the past several decades. (Courtesy of Brian Noe.)

Five

The Shareholders

In 1930, the State Parks Commission provided a report titled "Dividends on Connecticut State Parks: A Report to the Shareholders." Connecticut State Parks is a subsidiary company organized in 1913 by the state to provide open spaces for public recreation. The citizens of Connecticut receive one share each of Connecticut common stock, which since 1913 carries with it one share of state parks common. The commissioners believed that "the public is always willing to pay for services rendered, and that a State Park which is used can be made self-supporting, as other states have already proven."

Hammonasset did not have any authorized rules, regulations, or police to keep the peace until several years after the park opened. Imagine thousands of people on the beach and packing the campgrounds, overwhelming facilities and infrastructure yet somehow getting along.

Hammonasset mirrored the developments of society, including issues of liberty versus the protection of others. There was a consistent recognition of superior park services and amenities along with complaints. Some of the complaints stemmed from the mandate that the park be used in a wholesome and reasonable way. For example, the commissioners saw a need to provide a parking lot with a caretaker to watch over personal belongings. In the 1920s, there was a petition objecting to "the use of the beach by colored people." Card playing was prohibited, and strict bathing suit rules were challenged but not relaxed until the 1930s.

Many organizations also enjoyed Hammonasset, including disabled veterans, the Newington Home for Crippled Children, Hebrew Women's Home, and the Hartford Orphan Asylum, all looking to enjoy the beautiful Connecticut shoreline. Beach patrons and campers enjoyed wonderful services and amenities that soon became overwhelmed and run down due to tight budgets and were then repaired and expanded to a new level of excellence. This cycle continues to this day. As every sun rose and set, employees, visitors, and campers made the memories that make Hammonasset the cherished place it continues to be today.

Connecticut's population doubled from 1890 to 1920, creating crowded city conditions. People wanted to escape the crowds, noise, stifling summer temperatures without air conditioning, and the smells of inadequate sewage treatment. Hammonasset and other state parks were deserved by everyone.

Pictured is a fairly busy day in the first season of operations for Hammonasset. The reputation of the grand resort quickly boosted attendance, which overwhelmed the available bathhouses, locker space, and refectory. Sunday attendance in 1921 was topping 10,000 (many people worked on Saturdays). Visitors demanded additional facilities, and the commissioners were under pressure to meet demand, stave off criticism, and positively promote the park to the public and legislature.

This 1914 photograph shows the lighthouse and support buildings on Faulkner's Island. The lighthouse is a Hammonasset scenic highlight. The island was purchased and the lighthouse commissioned by Pres. Thomas Jefferson. It has been in near continuous use since before the War of 1812. (Courtesy of Jeremy D'Entremont, from the collection of Vivian Chapin.)

In 1921, Hammonasset produced a $5,000 surplus despite offering free entrance, parking, and weekend camping. Surpluses continued until the Depression, but by state statute, the legislature controlled the surplus, frustrating the commissioners' ability to manage the park from year to year. The Hammonasset Special was a mixture of hard-boiled eggs, Virginia baked ham, and mayonnaise served with lettuce and tomato on white bread.

Most visitors remained dressed in their Sunday best, including dresses and hats for the ladies and suits and hats for the gentlemen. Rental umbrellas provided some cover from the sun, as can be seen in this mid-1920s photograph.

Revenues were derived from refectory sales including clam chowder and the Hammonasset Perfecto cigar; rentals of swimsuits, umbrellas, towels, and lockers; and paid long-term camping. Rented swimsuits can be seen in this early 1920s photograph. Most of the rental swimsuits had a distinctive stripe. There were strict regulations regarding swimsuits. Men were required to wear tops, and neither gender was allowed to wear an open-back suit.

The beach takes on a different perspective in the winter. The winter of 1934 was unusually frigid, as can be seen by the frazil (soft ice formed in water that is too turbulent to freeze solid) in Long Island Sound.

The free parking lot behind the Grand Pavilion was busy on September 4, 1921, Labor Day weekend. Free parking continued until 1933, when the commissioners charged for parking to replace lost revenue from declining attendance, rentals, and sales at the park. Revenues were down 60 percent from 1927 to 1932. There were reports of resistance and failure to collect the parking fees.

Pictured on Labor Day weekend 1921, campers make use of the paid long-term camps on Dowd's Point Road (Beach Road). The commission allowed the park superintendent to lower camp fees for 1922 if increased volume would replace the lost revenue. By the end of 1922, low-volume camping was no longer an issue. Due to overwhelming demand, long-term campsites increased from 50 to 70 lots in 1923.

In 1925, the free short-term camps were expanded with improvements in lighting, water supply, and additional toilets. The $1,500 cost included improvements for the Dowd's (background) and Meigs Point camps. The Guilford-Chester Water Company supplied water to the park. Periodically, a combination of inadequate supply and infrastructure at Hammonasset, along with overwhelming demand, left toilets dry and steam boilers on watch for shutdown due to lack of water.

Roads were covered with calcium chloride to bind the grass and dirt and help vehicles drive in and out of parking lots and campgrounds. The ground held firm long enough for the summer season, with a new coating laid the following summer season. In 1929, the park laid gravel roads in the free weekend camps. Note the smoke from the campers cooking food.

The virtually empty short-term camps at left in 1927 (indicating a weekday) numbered 102 sites with additional overflow for weekends. There are no Chic Sales, and campers were able to use the bathhouses in the Administration Building. The $2,000 fenced-in paid parking lot for 400 cars (right) was created in 1923, and a caretaker watched the vehicles while visitors enjoyed their day at the beach. The white structures are changing stations. (Courtesy of MHS.)

In July 1923, Hammonasset purchased the first trial canvas bungalow for $250, to be set up at the Meigs Point camps. Tent camping was permitted as well. Eventually, 12 bungalows were erected with a weekly rental charge assessed. Weather took a toll on the canvas bungalows. There was a discussion to construct 14-by-20-foot, three-room bungalows made of poles and slabs with beaver board, but they were never built.

The bungalows were not profitable, as campers preferred to bring their own tents. This practice was growing so fast that rental camp equipment quickly came to an end. This 1927 aerial view shows the Meigs camp the last year bungalow rentals were offered to campers. The commissioners eyed Meigs as a place to expand camping, since they were considering converting Dowd's Point Road from long-term camping to day parking. (Courtesy of MHS.)

In 1930, the Meigs Point camps overflowed into the surrounding fields, beyond any conveniences. This did not make for happy campers and was a public health issue. The 1936 Meigs Point camp maps 121 sites plus room for overflow campers. A road was rebuilt to Dowd's Island for future camping, and campsites along the Hammonasset River were considered. Willard's Island was not developed for camping in the 1930s.

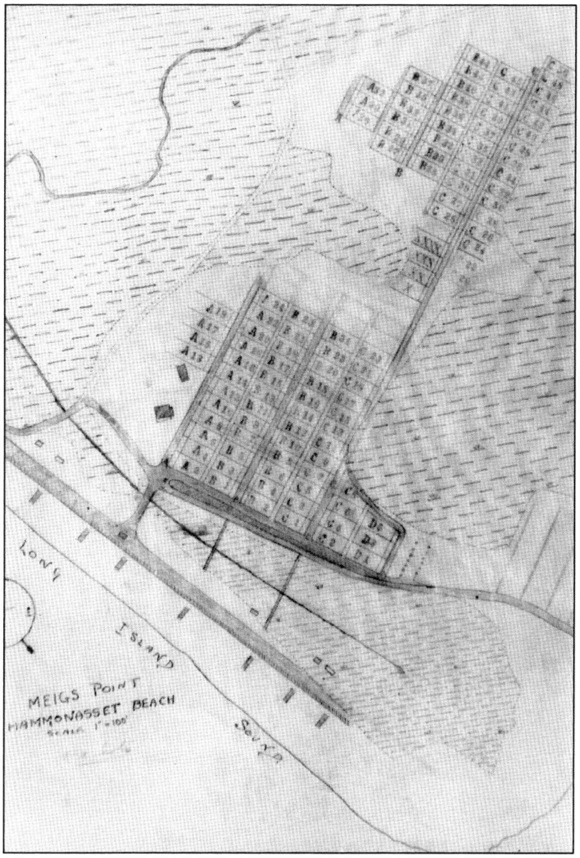

This 1922 view of Dowd's Point Road was taken from the Grand Pavilion.

The Dowd's long-term camps in 1927 were expanded to 78 Dowd's Point Road lots and 60 lots on what are now O and P Streets. Campsite roads were two-lane boulevards. Each campsite had its own outhouse. Narrow roads behind the outhouses were for the "honey wagon" (waste collector) to swap out the buckets used by the campers. Note the boardwalk from the Meigs Cottage to Dowd's Point Road. (Courtesy of MHS.)

Reservations were made by mail for long-term campsites. In 1929, there were only about 200 sites in both the Dowd's and Meigs Point camps. That year, 60 sites were reserved by January 3, creating a call to action for the commission to create more camps. The Dowd's long-term camps were virtually full every summer with portable houses, trailers, and tents. This photograph was probably taken on a weekday, since there are few cars at campsites and the day visitor parking is nearly empty.

In 1931, a road was built across Tom's Creek, adding four new circle camps. Area I started with 64 campsites, but due to overcrowding, the number of sites was reduced to 48, with convenient arrangement of toilets, lights, and water. The white patch could be where the fill came from for the road. Budget constraints ended camping on Labor Day weekend during the Depression.

This 1936 map depicts the Dowd and Area I long-term camps. The 16-site-per-circle camps established in 1931 proved to be too tight and were reduced to 12 sites per circle. The circles were given local Native American names: Tunxis (Farmington area), Mohican (western New England), Pequot (a warlike tribe neighboring and attacking the Quinnipiac), and Montowese (a Quinnipiac or Wangunk tribe in the North Haven area).

Over 600 short-term and 197 Dowd's long-term campsites were packed on July 4, 1937. Expansion in 1931 required upgrades in water supply (a consistent issue), toilets, and lighting. Including 120 Meigs Point long-term campsites, Hammonasset now offered over 900 equipped campsites plus overflow camping. The drainage canal from Dowd's Creek to Tom's Creek was constructed in 1935. Chestnut poles to deliver electricity, set in 1920, were in dangerous condition. Underground wiring for electricity and telephone lines was installed. The six-inch wooden water pipe needed emergency replacement in 1936. Funding was primarily from federal aid, but relief work was concentrated in population centers. Hammonasset was not a population center, and failed to gain relief, leaving work partially completed with no prospect for resumption. A camper complaint in 1937 to the Connecticut Board of Health regarding sanitary conditions at campsites led to an inspection and order for improvements.

Campers and beach patrons were frequently pestered by mosquitoes and green flies. The commission made mosquito control a top priority by budgeting laborers to use a ditch digger (shown here by Russ Miller and on display at the Meigs Point Nature Center) to carve trenches in the marsh. This allowed small fish to feed on mosquito larvae. This backbreaking work continued into the 1950s, when machines took over the drudgery. (Courtesy of Shelby Docker.)

Outhouses were sometimes referred to as Chic Sales from the 1930s into the 1950s. Chic Sale was a well-known vaudeville comedian who wrote *The Specialist*, a play about an outhouse builder named Lem Putt. The play and later his adapted book became very popular, especially in the 1930s. Notice the quad (four-door) Chic Sale at lower right next to the car. There was one door on each side to accommodate four campsites.

A petition signed by 160 campers was presented to the commission by an attorney objecting to the 28-day camping limit on Connecticut residents in January 1938. The commission was seeking to accommodate high demand for the long-term camps. The commissioners responded by restricting campers who used long-term sites for weekend parties, to limit nonresident campers to 15 camp days, and to postpone the 28-day limit for resident campers. Relieving the long-term camper congestion, the rule was carried over into 1939. Superintendent Parker did not like the idea after receiving complaints from nonresidents. For the 1940 camp season, Connecticut residents could mail in reservations on a first-come, first-served basis effective March 1. The date for nonresident reservations was June 15. This effectively ended nonresident long-term camping, since the long-term sites were full, leading to the development of Dud's and Young's village. Fees for camping in 1937 were reduced from 60¢ to 50¢ per day.

This rare winter photograph shows the Grand Pavilion. Imagine how cold it must be in there on a windy day with snow adding that extra chill.

Snow graces the men's bathhouse. This photograph was taken a year before the 1938 hurricane.

The Curtiss Aerocar fifth-wheel trailer, dubbed the "Caddy of Campers" due to its craftsmanship and beauty, was constructed along aeroframe principles, believed to be priced between $2,000 and $6,000 depending on model and options. Curtiss was touted as the first to offer a 110-volt air conditioner for $199. These trailers were not typically seen at Hammonasset. Notice the homemade campers in the background in contrast to this beauty. (Courtesy of Gail Najarian.)

In 1937, the Henry Hill family of New Britain camped at Hammonasset in this impressive example of a homemade camper built by Hill. He converted a large horse trailer, built on the roof of the Fair Building, a five-and-dime store in New Britain. He lowered each piece from the roof. (Courtesy of Gail Najarian.)

This is a view of Henry Hill's custom kitchen, set up in the back of the trailer, decorated with plaid curtains, a light and electrical fixture, and fruit on the counter. Notice the wood cabinets, ice chest, and the all-important brass fire extinguisher mounted to the cabinet at lower left. (Courtesy of Gail Najarian.)

This "living room area" is on the front side of Henry Hill's custom camper. It was decorated with matching plaid curtains, a light fixture, an electrical outlet, and an upholstered couch that spanned the width of the camper, providing comfort in the family's home away from home. (Courtesy of Gail Najarian.)

Although lacking legal authority for enforcement, Hammonasset had fairly strict regulations. General regulations included no alcohol, no card playing of any sort (changed to no gambling of any sort in 1933), dogs must be on a leash at all times (changed in 1933 to between April 15 and October 15), no "digs" (carving structures or trees with initials and so on, authorized in 1933), and keg beer was prohibited in 1934. Beach regulations included no ball playing, beach fires, dressing on the beach, tents, or screens; jerseys must be worn outside of tights (except for California suits starting in 1929), dressing in cars was not allowed (a $1 fine and eviction reduced the problem in the 1930s), no glass or crockery on the beach, no sun-back bathing suits, and men must wear bathing suit tops (suspended in 1939). Perhaps all these rules made the little girl above run across the beach crying.

By 1927, the commissioners greatly expanded and made improvements at Hammonasset. However, as can be seen in this July 1927 pavilion photograph, overwhelming crowds, continuing to exceed 10,000 on a Sunday, queued up to rent 4,000 lockers, along with swimsuits, towels, umbrellas, and other items. There were similar lines to purchase food and beverages. The commissioners simply did not have the funding to meet the demand of the 1920s.

Lifeguards and staff did an outstanding job ensuring public safety. Lifeguards watched for bathers in distress and enforced safety from elevated chairs and rowboats on the water. In 1929, the first outboard motor was purchased, seen at right in this 1939 photograph. The lifeguards rescued 20 to 45 swimmers a year. Lifeguards and nurses also treated 400 to 1,700 injuries per season.

Benches instead of fencing made for a more natural beach setting and were a practical amenity for people to enjoy their day at the beach. Park staff planted poison ivy and small marsh alder, shrubs that can still be found today, where the boardwalk and benches did not provide protection from trampling.

There were several claims for damages involving injuries at the park in the 1920s and 1930s. In every case, the commission determined that the circumstances did not seem to suggest negligence by the state and that the state was not liable for such accidents. In addition, the commission had no power to use funds for that purpose.

With the entire two-mile beach, seen in this 1927 aerial view, easily accessible to the public from Tom's Creek to Meigs Point in 1931, people had alternatives to the overcrowded pavilion area. The commissioners considered the one-mile reserve beach along the Hammonasset River for future development. (Courtesy of MHS.)

Sailors enjoy the smooth waters of Long Island Sound at Hammonasset Beach in 1936. Today, dozens of sailboats, motor boats, kayaks, and paddle boarders can be seen on any nice day at Hammonasset. (Courtesy of Jeff Barske.)

The sand where the Harlow, Smith, and Hill Cottages stood in 1930 was pushed back to the level of the concrete seawall to create a safe area for cooking fires elevated above and separated from the beach at the water's edge for the 1931 summer season. The property owners built the concrete wall to protect their cottages. Note the man jumping off the seawall.

A large area behind the Harlow, Smith, and Hills Cottages was fit out with toilets and running water for use by one-day campers. This allowed people with children to pitch a tent to use as a dressing shelter and have a well-equipped picnic place for a day's pleasure.

It was not unusual for visitors dressed to the nines to visit the refectory to sample the renowned Hammonasset clam chowder. Note the fur-collared coat on the gentleman and the dress on the young lady in this 1941 photograph.

A pet seal is pictured in the 1930s. It is not known who coaxed this seal into becoming a pet, but hopefully it was only temporary before releasing it back into the wild. (Courtesy of CLEMA.)

This photograph of the *Hindenburg* over Hammonasset heading to Lakehurst Naval Air Station, New Jersey, from Frankfurt, Germany, was taken by state park employee Bill Miller in August 1936, its first year of transatlantic service. According to the diary of Clarence and Dorothy Hall of Philadelphia, this flight probably included attendees of the 1936 Olympics and celebrities including German boxer Max Schmeling, who defeated Joe Lewis at sold-out Yankee Stadium in June; Schmeling's trainer, Max Machon; and movie star Douglas Fairbanks and his new wife, Lady Sylvia Ashley. Capt. Ernst Lehmann flew the Halls over their home in Philadelphia before landing at Lakehurst. Altitude during the trip was 400 to 6,000 feet and the zeppelin flew at 75 miles per hour. A one-way fare was $400. The *Hindenburg's* last flight ended in disaster on May 6, 1937, in Lakehurst.

Oliver and Gladys Scory, seen camping in the early 1930s, began a decades-long tradition of Hammonasset camping with their young sons, Ray and Bobby. Ray and Jane Emirzian Docker met again at Hammonasset in the 1960s and married in 1976, camping with Jane's children, John and Shelby Docker. Camping and visiting Hammonasset is a tradition for many families, including the authors. (Courtesy of Raymond Scory.)

Gladys Hill was a resident of New Britain camping at Hammonasset with her family as long-term campers. Gladys is pictured enjoying the day at the beach in 1927 with her daughter, Betty Hill Tattersall, who also camped at Hammonasset with her family. Betty's daughter Gail Tattersall Najarian continued the tradition, also camping at Hammonasset with her family for decades. (Courtesy of Gail Najarian.)

The Vine, along River Road near today's Interstate 95, was a popular spot to jump off rope swings and swim in the Hammonasset River. It was enjoyed by the authors for many years in the 1970s and was a popular place to hang out in the 1930s. Note the bike along the road railing. (Courtesy of Jeff Barske.)

Men and boys did not have to wear shirts when outside of Hammonasset Beach, as seen by the tan lines of, from left to right, Lester Bloomberg, Ed Conway, Dave Tyler, and Jimmy Gross standing on a rock in the Hammonasset River in 1938. (Courtesy of Jeff Barske.)

Women did not have to wear tights to cover their thighs when outside of Hammonasset Beach. From left to right, Shirley Barske, Kathy ?, Beth ?, Dottie ?, and Miggs Barske stand on a rock in the Hammonasset River in 1938. Note the railroad trestle behind them. I-95 would be constructed behind the trestle in the 1950s. (Courtesy of Jeff Barske.)

Children loved to go crabbing and fishing on the many bridges that spanned the drainage canal, Tom's Creek, Dudley's Creek, and anywhere else crabs dared to roam. Bobby Scory (left), age three, and Ray Scory (center), age five, pose for a photograph in 1940 for their father, Oliver Scory. (Courtesy of Raymond Scory.)

Many campers arrived at Hammonasset with a trailer, probably homemade; a tent and furnishings (probably from their home); and utensils and supplies. This family is obviously big fans of Tom Thumb, an English fairy tale first published in 1621. A stork delivered the thumb-sized baby who aged but did not grow. The adventures began when Tom ventured into the outside world. A Tom Thumb cartoon movie released in 1936 may have been the impetus to create Camp Tom Thumb. This family set up in the short-term camp.

A camper tradition for many decades was the Labor Day Parade. Every parade needs a marching band, as seen in 1936 (above) and 1941 (below). (Below, courtesy of Gail Najarian.)

People dressed in crazy attire, including "Mr. Kitchen Gadget" and "Balloon Woman." There were prizes for the best costumes. (Both, courtesy of Gail Najarian.)

Above, two young girls march with the color guard. The parades drew a good crowd. Some people just didn't seem to get excited about the Labor Day Parade, especially when dressed up as Cupid (right). (Both, courtesy of Gail Najarian.)

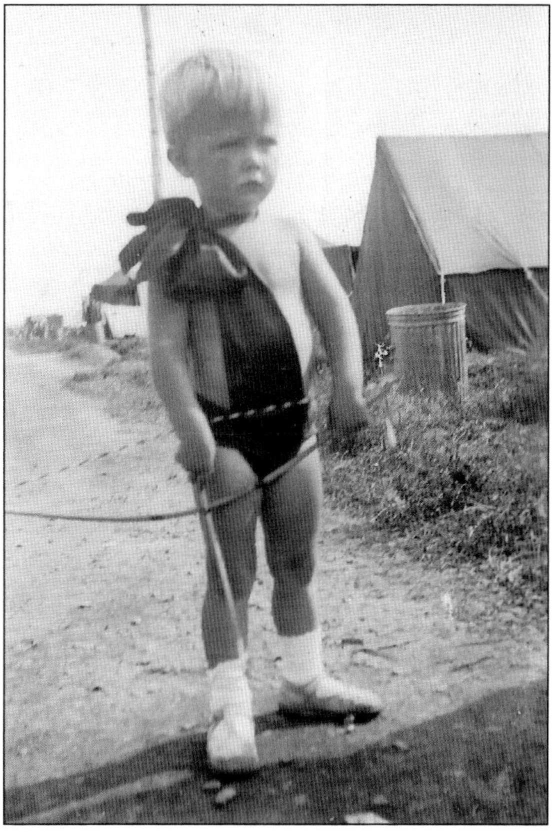

Hammonasset survived the historic flood of 1936 in relatively good shape compared to the rest of New England, where it left at least 150 dead, thousands homeless, and over $100 million in damage. This flood photograph was taken on the east side of the Administration Building facing the Clam Shed. Note the assembly and garage building on the high ground of Cedar Knoll on the left.

An above-average snowfall and a stalled warm front on March 9, 1936, brought 14 days of rain, leading to widespread flooding and destruction. The vision to build elevated structures at Hammonasset paid off in spades that would keep on giving 30 months later. This flood photograph was taken from the boardwalk facing the Dowd's Camp. The bathhouse and lockers of the Administration Building are at left.

Six

The 1938 Hurricane and World War II

There was little warning when the "Long Island Express" (hurricanes were not officially named until 1950) struck Connecticut on September 21, 1938. Fortunately, it made landfall on an autumn weekday with few visitors and the camps shut down due to budget constraints from the Depression. The photographs in this chapter cannot capture the full emotional distress of the worst hurricane to ever hit New England. The determination of the staff to rebuild the park structures for the 1939 summer season can only be appreciated through the photographs of the completed and improved park facilities.

The hurricane of 1938 was followed by the occupation of the park by the US Army Air Force during World War II, which temporarily closed the park until 1945. Hammonasset was open to day visitors in the summer of 1942, but camping was banned due to blackout rules for protection against German U-boats. In November 1942, the US Army leased the park from the commission. There was a discussion to keep the western part of Hammonasset open, since the Army wanted the eastern side and Meigs Point to be used for fighter aircraft target training, but it was determined that the danger of having civilians so close to the training area was not worth the benefit of keeping part of the park open. There are also reports, but no definitive proof, that soldiers practiced beach landings on Hammonasset Beach.

When Hammonasset was released back to the commissioners, it was surprising that most of the damage to the park was done by vandals, not the Army, despite having night watchmen on patrol (a practice started in the early 1920s to ward off trespassers).

The beginning of World War II was the end of an era marked by the vision, determination, longevity, and continuity of the commissioners, staff, and patrons of Hammonasset Beach State Park. They withstood challenges and had little luck, but prevailed to provide the best possible experience for visitors of Hammonasset, which continues to stand the test of time.

The state commissioned aerial photographs two days after the September 21, 1938, Long Island Express hurricane to assess the damage. The structures were solid enough to repair with long-planned but delayed improvements for the park's reopening on May 11, 1939. A plan to replace the chestnut posts with concrete in 1935 didn't materialize. Perhaps the resiliency of the wood structures put that idea to rest for good.

Tides were 10 feet over normal levels with "the extreme high water of about 12' and the board walk went with it," according to commission minutes. Here, park staff inspect the destruction of the buildings, boardwalk, and what little is left of the dunes. Initial repair estimates of $50,000 quickly became $126,224, including road repair. The request to the governor included full funding by April 1, 1939, to open the park for the summer season.

Large sections of boardwalk rest against the Grand Pavilion. The destroyed ramps and missing boardwalk expose the support structures of the pavilion that survived the sustained winds of well over 100 miles per hour, the highest on record. Note the partial breach in the beach under the center entrance, perhaps the Long Island Sound attempting to reclaim the marsh.

It is remarkable that the Grand Pavilion repairs and improvements were completed in time for the summer 1939 beach season. Notice the new side ramps funneling pedestrian movement from each end of the pavilion to the center onto the new, wider, extended boardwalk.

"Ghost posts" stand as silent sentinels between the Grand Pavilion and the waves of the Long Island Sound. The protective dunes were no match for the winds and 12-foot-plus storm surge. The foresight and vision of the commissioners and park staff to build elevated structures may have saved the buildings from complete destruction.

An up-close view illustrates damage where light comes through the missing rear portion of the roof of the Grand Pavilion, which was literally blown away. The superintendent used existing dead chestnut wood poles from Devil's Hopyard, another state park in East Haddam, to build the pavilion. The posts underneath appear to be unmoved by the hurricane.

The Grand Pavilion is seen with new side ramps and the clock prominently placed where it was before the hurricane. The clock reads 2:25 on this sunny afternoon. The sign below states the date, Saturday, July 8, probably the water temperature, and times for high and low tides. Picnic tables along the beach side of the pavilion provide shade, a place to eat, and a great place for people watching.

This photograph was taken from the west side of the newly constructed Grand Pavilion ramp with a view looking out at the summer crowd toward Meigs Point. The wider boardwalk promenade shows beachgoers in swimsuits mixed with fully clothed men and women enjoying the day at the beach, truly a place for everyone. Men were allowed to forego swim tops for the first time in 1939.

This aerial view shows that the Administration Building survived relatively intact due to its enclosed wall construction. The wind was not able to whip through the building like it did on the open floor plan of the Grand Pavilion or bathhouse, where part of the roof was blow away. Is it a fluke of nature that the boardwalk on the east side of the first aid station survived?

This photograph faces the Administration Building and Clam Shed. In April 1939, the park superintendent requested authority to proceed at the earliest possible moment with additional work that needed to be done at Hammonasset. His estimates included $23,360 for 7,300 linear feet of eight-foot-wide boardwalk and $3,000 for surfacing the boardwalk. The legislature passed House Bill 650 on May 3, appropriating $50,000 for the rehabilitation of Hammonasset.

This photograph from the roof of the Grand Pavilion shows (in the foreground) the rebuilt ramp to the parking lot, the new ramp on the west side of the Administration Building to the first aid station and men's bathhouse, and the entrance to the administration offices. Note the beach visitor with a shade umbrella.

The unmistakable Red Cross flag flying in the breeze identifies the first aid station from the beach and boardwalk. Nurses liked to sit in the shade next to the entrance to the women's bathhouse on the east side of the Administration Building. Note the poles at the edge of the ramp to the footpath leading to the parking lot, designed to keep vehicles off of the boardwalk.

This photograph shows how the renowned open-air Clam Shed suffered significant damage and beach erosion from the hurricane. The right side of the outdoor deck and picnic table are gone. The storm surge and rough surf hit these vulnerable structures, which were built on slightly lower marshland.

Outdoor picnic tables balance precariously on partially collapsed decking, with the smashed boardwalk offering some support. A man can be seen at upper right sitting on a picnic table. Most of the fixed picnic tables under the cover of the roof survived the storm.

On the west side of the Clam Shed, two poles with light fixtures and attached wires survived the hurricane slightly askew. The boardwalk, in a pile of rubble, was not as fortunate. By February 1939, the park superintendent purchased pile-driving equipment to rebuild the boardwalk. He also ordered white cedar piles from the Pachaug Forest, another Connecticut state park.

Clam chowder was ready to be served by the 1939 summer season. A new center entrance ramp replaced the stairs on the Clam Shed. The ramp to the beach was shortened to adjust for the narrow beach due to erosion from the hurricane.

Dowd's Creek was reunited with Long Island Sound for the first time in park history due to the hurricane. It is believed that Dowd's Creek was cut off from the sound by natural forces in the 1890s. The men's bathhouse is missing part of the east side of the roof. Both the men's and women's bathhouses suffered significant damage to the boardwalk and ramps.

This aerial photograph taken over land shows how the hurricane pushed the sand over the flattened dunes into the short-term camp area. The hole in the roof of the men's bathhouse is easily visible.

The hurricane-force winds caused devastating damage to cottages on Shore Road in Clinton, just two and a half miles east of Hammonasset, reinforcing the thought that if the park commission had not moved the six cottages along the beachfront, they may have been destroyed also.

The administration buildings on Cedar Knoll (behind today's Mohegan and Podunk camp circles) survived relatively intact. One has to wonder if the Smith, Harlow, and Hills Cottages would have been destroyed if not moved off the beach to Cedar Knoll.

In October 1939, construction began on the boardwalk extension east from the bathhouses to the picnic area, formerly the location of the Smith, Harlow, and Hills Cottages. Discussions in 1935 to replace the wooden boardwalk with one made of gravel did not bear fruit, but gravel walkways were used on Meigs Point Road.

From the shadows in this photograph, this is a morning work crew on the boardwalk with the pile driver. This extension was designed differently from the original boardwalk that extended from the Grand Pavilion to the bathhouses.

Compare this photograph with the one below to identify the distinct difference of this design with the traditional-style boardwalk post and railings. The posts buried in the sand and extended above the walkway without side rails appeared more substantial and better able to weather storms.

The rebuilt main boardwalk and ramps to the men's and women's bathhouses were similar to the original design with railings and benches. When the boardwalk was rebuilt, the light poles were placed on the beach side of the boardwalk. The pitched ramp in the foreground leads to the parking lot.

Using diagonal spaces along Meigs Point Road allowed for additional parking. More parking accommodated more people at this popular stretch of beach, as can be seen on this busy day in 1932. Vegetated barrier dunes, including poison ivy and marsh alder, helped to keep patrons off the dunes and enjoying the sand and surf.

In contrast to the photograph above, the hurricane completely wiped out the Meigs Point Road, dunes, and ramps to the beach all the way to Meigs Point. There was criticism that placing the Meigs Point Road so close to the shore failed to adequately protect the beach and infrastructure. The manager's house (the old nature center) and both barns survived with minimal damage.

This photograph taken from the manager's cottage porch shows the newly rebuilt Meigs Point Road ready for the 1939 summer season. The entrance and booth to the Meigs camp was moved to the east (left) of the manager's cottage. Note the larger Chic Sales erected to accommodate this popular stretch of beach. The tradition of parking right in front of the dunes continued until well past World War II.

Belmont Scofield, president of the Campers and Trailers Association, appeared at the commissioners' meeting at Hammonasset in July 1939 to submit a petition for improvements including that a boardwalk from Dowd's Point be installed at once. A catwalk was built in July and August, to be followed by more permanent construction. The catwalk ran from the campers' beach at the end of Dowd's Point Road to the Grand Pavilion.

This aerial photograph shows portable houses in Young's Village off Dudley Road to the north of Hammonasset that were hit hard. The Dudley House, owned by the park commission and still standing, is above the portable houses to the right. The Young House is at right in front of the road leading to the portable houses. Dowd's Point Road can be seen at upper left.

This ground-level photograph shows the destruction seen above. Note that one portable house made it through relatively unscathed. The car on the left appears to be the same car in the same location as in the aerial view above. Perhaps the photographs were taken within hours or days of each other. (Courtesy of Gail Najarian.)

This 1939 view from the top of the Grand Pavilion shows Dowd's and Area I full of campers. The boardwalk from the Grand Pavilion parking lot through the marsh to Dowd's Point Road is gone, destroyed by the hurricane. Notice the repairs to the pavilion's paper roofing.

Camping was back to normal in 1939 on Meigs Point, with everything from portable houses to campers and tents. Note the campsites stretching back to the entrance of today's Cedar Island Trail and to the marsh on the far eastern side of the park. Beyond the tree line and marsh is the Clinton Harbor and mouth and inlet to the Hammonasset River.

The boardwalk extended west toward Meigs Point, past the picnic area, with a parking lot on the left in 1941. The line of Chic Sales is visible along the rebuilt Meigs Point Road and beach in the background.

This photograph, taken in 1939 or later, shows a breach on the beach, another reuniting of Dowd's Creek with Long Island Sound. Note the short ramps to the very narrow beach at what is likely a higher than normal high tide. Grasses are hung up in the fencing under the boardwalk. (Courtesy of Gail Najarian.)

This view of Dowd's Point Road was taken from the campers' beach. Note the ramp that led to the beach and a catwalk to the main boardwalk, pavilion, and other buildings. Portable houses were very popular as World War II approached and would continue to grow in popularity after the war.

People enjoy a day at the Meigs Point beach in 1940. Note the rebuilt gravel sidewalk, posts, and Chic Sales after the 1938 hurricane in the background. Visitors were able to park right on the beach, a practice criticized by some as exposing the beach to storm damage without a protective dune barrier. This exposure would be corrected after World War II. (Courtesy of Jeff Barske.)

Hammonasset was open to daytime use only during the summer of 1942. Camping was prohibited along the entire shoreline due to blackout restrictions put in place by the military. Attendance was down 25 to 50 percent at all state parks. Parking fees were scaled back to weekends only—fees collected on weekdays did not cover the cost of collection. The Army took over Hammonasset in November 1942.

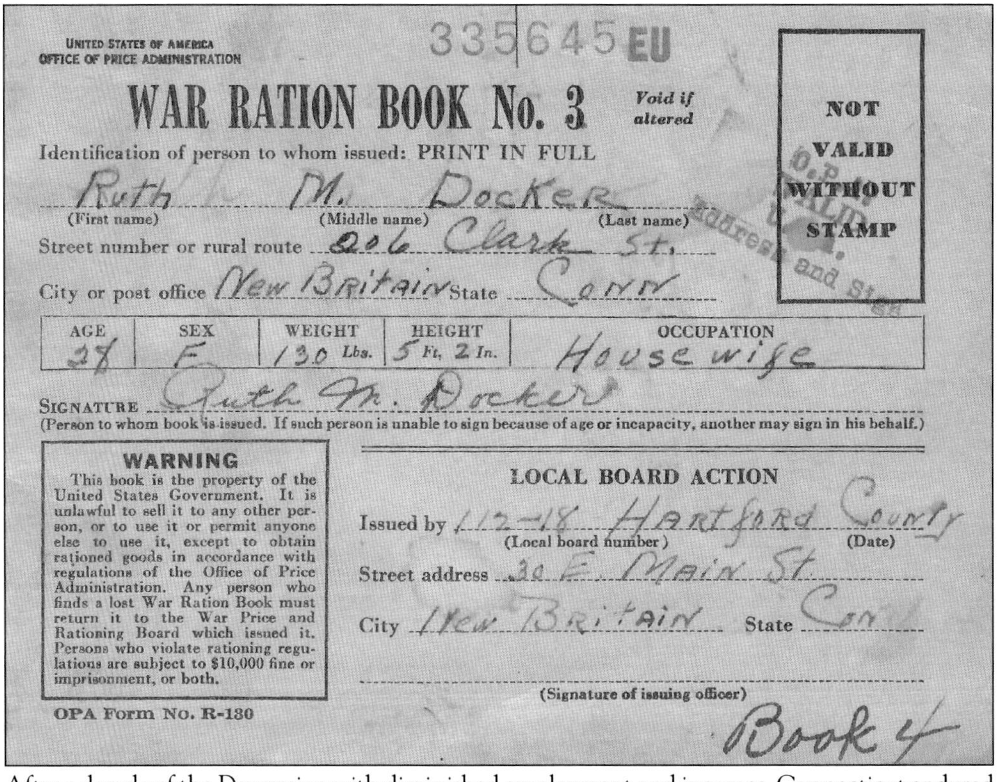

UNITED STATES OF AMERICA
OFFICE OF PRICE ADMINISTRATION

335645 EU

WAR RATION BOOK No. 3 *Void if altered*

NOT VALID WITHOUT STAMP

Identification of person to whom issued: PRINT IN FULL

Ruth M. Docker
(First name) (Middle name) (Last name)

Street number or rural route 206 Clark St.

City or post office New Britain State Conn

AGE	SEX	WEIGHT	HEIGHT	OCCUPATION
28	F	130 Lbs.	5 Ft. 2 In.	Housewife

SIGNATURE Ruth M. Docker
(Person to whom book is issued. If such person is unable to sign because of age or incapacity, another may sign in his behalf.)

WARNING
This book is the property of the United States Government. It is unlawful to sell it to any other person, or to use it or permit anyone else to use it, except to obtain rationed goods in accordance with regulations of the Office of Price Administration. Any person who finds a lost War Ration Book must return it to the War Price and Rationing Board which issued it. Persons who violate rationing regulations are subject to $10,000 fine or imprisonment, or both.

OPA Form No. R-130

LOCAL BOARD ACTION

Issued by 1-12-18 Hartford County
(Local board number) (Date)

Street address 30 E. Main St

City New Britain State Con

(Signature of issuing officer)

Book 4

After a decade of the Depression with diminished employment and incomes, Connecticut endured rationing as did most of the world's population during World War II. Tires, gasoline, and sugar were rationed in 1942. Many other commodities were soon rationed or were simply not available. This war ration book was for Ruth Docker, Shelby Docker's grandmother. Night courts were established to enforce the gasoline rationing rule, often violated by sightseeing drivers. (Courtesy of Shelby Docker.)

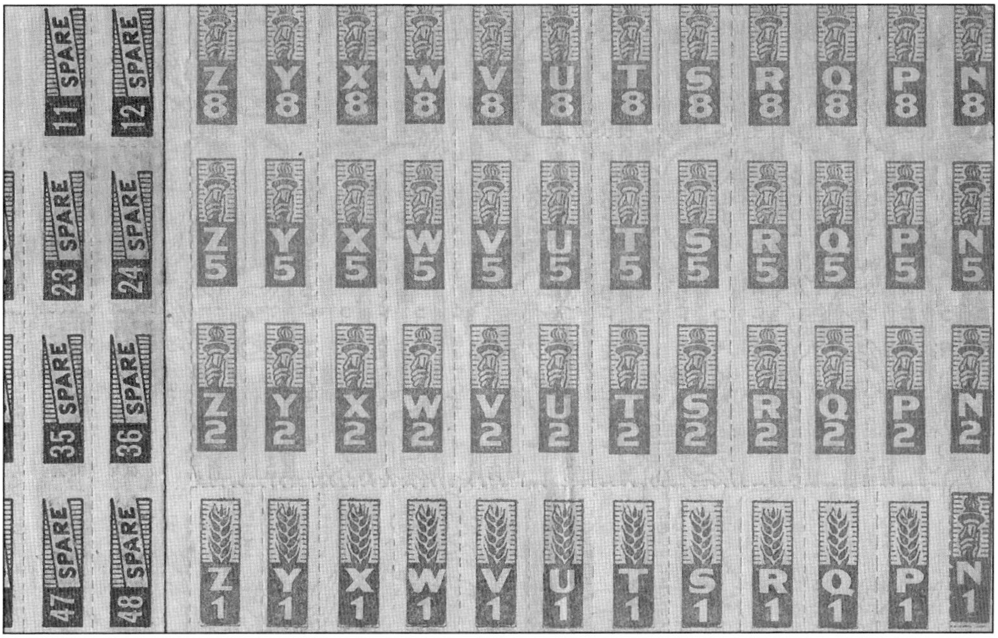

Goods a person could receive were defined by the stamps contained in the ration book. Letters and numbers determined the amount of stamps to cover the price of specific goods. The value of the letters and numbers periodically changed. It is difficult to imagine that Hammonasset would have had many visitors with gasoline rationing, and if it did, if food and beverage would have been available at the park.

Republic P-47B Thunderbolt fighter planes fly in formation, with Hammonasset Beach seen to the right of plane 16002 and Clinton Harbor seen over the nose of the same aircraft. This is one of the first photographs released to the public of these airplanes. Well over 20,000 P-47s were produced during the war, about half on Long Island in Farmingdale, New York. (Courtesy of the Clinton Historical Society.)

P-47s flew over Clinton Harbor to practice strafing along the beach of Hammonasset before flying toward Faulkner's Island. These seven .50-caliber casings, from Frankford and St. Louis Arsenals between 1941 and 1943, and two 20-millimeter casings were found near the Meigs Point picnic shelter. It is reported that German prisoners of war helped to clean the beach of spent and sometimes live ordnance. (Courtesy of Paul Edman and CLEMA.)

The commissioners accepted settlement of damages by the US Army on June 13, 1945. Most of the damage was done by vandals. Part of the park, in need of repairs, was available for use by the public on June 28. The Meigs Point Road and camps were still closed as of August 17, 1945, not to reopen until 1946. Note the two antennae on Meigs Point. (Courtesy of Jeff Barske.)

About the Organization

The Park

Hammonasset Beach State Park is on the shore of Long Island Sound in Madison, Connecticut. In addition to Connecticut's largest shoreline park, with over two miles of beach to enjoy, visitors will find wetlands and woodlands. People come to the park to walk, bike, kayak, swim, fish, study nature, bird watch, picnic, or just relax. Hammonasset offers over 550 grassy campsites as well as several rustic cabins.

The Friends

Friends of Hammonasset is a nonprofit 501(c)(3) volunteer organization, working in cooperation with state and local park management and the Friends of Connecticut State Parks. The purpose of the organization is to provide environmental education, preserve the integrity of the Hammonasset Beach State Park's natural resources, and serve as an advocate for the park.

Meigs Point Nature Center

Meigs Point Nature Center is an exciting and vital environmental learning center open to all ages at Hammonasset Beach State Park, one of the most beautiful sites within the Connecticut state park system. The interior of the nature center, as well as many of the programs offered there, are funded through donations from the Friends of Hammonasset.

Events

The Friends of Hammonasset hold several fundraising events each year. Every dollar is important and goes directly to park events, education, and facility enhancements. There is an online option for those who would like to contribute. Help us reach our goal of preserving and protecting Hammonasset Beach State Park while educating the general public and local community on this natural and cultural resource.

Learn more at www.friendsofhammonasset.org